3RD EDITION

saying WHEN

HOW TO QUIT DRINKING OR CUT DOWN

MARTHA SANCHEZ-CRAIG

FOREWORD BY WILLIAM R. MILLER

* Previously published as DrinkWise

camh

Centre for Addiction and Mental Health

A Pan American Health Organization /
World Health Organization Collaborating Centre

Library and Archives Canada Cataloguing in Publication

Sanchez-Craig, Martha, 1935-
     Saying when : how to quit drinking or cut down / Martha Sanchez-Craig. -- 3rd ed., rev.

Issued also in French under the title: C'est assez!
Issued also in electronic format.
ISBN 978-1-77052-904-5

     1. Temperance. 2. Controlled drinking. 3. Alcoholism-- Prevention. I. Centre for Addiction and
Mental Health II. Title.

HV5278.S26 2012   362.29'28   C2011-908051-6

ISBN: 978-1-77052-904-5 (PRINT)
ISBN: 978-1-77052-905-2 (PDF)
ISBN: 978-1-77052-905-2 (HTML)
ISBN: 978-1-77052-907-6 (ePUB)

Printed in Canada

Previously published as *DrinkWise*
Copyright © 1993, 1994, 1995, 2013, Centre for Addiction and Mental Health

This publication may be available in other formats. For information about alternate formats or
other CAMH publications, or to place an order, please contact Sales and Distribution:
Toll-free: 1 800 661-1111
Toronto: 416 595-6059
E-mail: publications@camh.net
Online store: http://store.camh.net

Website: www.camh.net

Disponible en français sous le titre : *C'est assez!*

4330 /03-2013 / PG081

Contents

Acknowledgments

I am grateful to the hundreds of clients who participated in our clinical trials, and to the Addiction Research Foundation (ARF)* for supporting the entire body of research. A grant from the National Institute of Alcohol and Alcoholism (NIAAA) in the United States also helped. But, to a large extent, it was the collaboration of so many colleagues that made the research program possible.

First, I would like to thank Keith Walker, who struggled with me in the initial project starting in 1973, involving clients with severe alcohol problems. His input in the formulation of our cognitive model of heavy alcohol use was invaluable. I also thank Carole Bush and Carol Broom for teaching clients the goal-setting and coping strategies that are key in our program. I appreciate the tenacity of Ken Sproule in locating clients at follow-up, which greatly increased the quality of this study.

From 1977 to 1995, we focused on "early" intervention for clients with mild to moderate alcohol problems. Some colleagues joined me as therapists, among them Ken Macdonald, Karen Spivak, Tony Hunt, Carole Bush, Larry Emens-Jelinek and Adrian Wilkinson. I thank them all for lending their clinical skills to the development of the program. I am indebted to Yedi Israel and Adrian Wilkinson for their recommendation to include liver and cognitive tests in our intake and follow-up assessments. These tests validated the drinking measures and increased the quality of our studies. Our high follow-up rates are due in large part to Virginia Ittig-Deland and Antonella Bianca. I am grateful for their persistence in locating clients and getting their information. Richard Bornet and Rafaela Davila were meticulous

* In 1998, the Centre for Addiction and Mental Health was created by the merging of the Addiction Research Foundation, the Clarke Institute of Psychiatry, the Donwood Institute and the Queen Street Mental Health Centre.

in organizing and analyzing the abundance of data gathered from hundreds of clients. Hau Lei provided expert advice on statistical analysis and was instrumental in establishing our guidelines for sensible drinking. I am grateful for the assistance of Rafaela Davila and Gerry Cooper while evaluating *Saying When* in rural and remote communities of Northern Ontario, and for the assistance of Gillian Leigh and Karen Spivak in the production of earlier versions of the self-help guide.

Over 22 years the research produced four formats of the program:
· Counselling — As described in the *Therapist's Manual*
· Advice — "Guidelines for Sensible Drinking"
· Self-help — *Saying When*
· Education program — DrinkWise*

I am grateful to the ARF for supporting many invitations to present our treatment methods and research findings in numerous international conferences and within Canada, and for allowing me to spend research time with psychologists and physicians who wanted to learn our methods at the Hjellestad Clinic in Bergen, Norway, and Hospital Mãe de Deus in Porto Alegre, Brazil. I valued the evaluation of the Guidelines by the late Jandira Masur and her team at Escola Paulista de Medicina in São Paulo, Brazil. Under the leadership of Yedi Israel, the Guidelines were evaluated in a project involving physicians and nurses in Cambridge, Ontario. Dr. Doug Wilson from the College of Family Physicians of Canada used them in a project with family doctors. I thank them all for contributing to the research.

* The DrinkWise education format was created by myself, Adrian Wilkinson and Karen Spivak in the early 1990s to satisfy a collaborative agreement between ARF and Homewood Health Services in Guelph, Ontario. The agreement was later dissolved, and Homewood became the owner this format. Unlike the other three formats, which we evaluated using rigorous scientific methodology, *DrinkWise*, as offered through Homewood, was not evaluated in our research program. The DrinkWise education format has proliferated in various parts of Canada and the United States.

Acknowledgments

My very special gratitude goes to my spouse, Adrian Wilkinson, who supported me emotionally and intellectually. His persistent encouragement helped me to endure difficult times, but what I mostly treasure is his ability to clarify the expression of my ideas.

I am grateful to Michelle Maynes, in Knowledge and Innovation Support at CAMH, for her editorial comments and dedication in the production of this new edition.

I would also like to acknowledge the thoughtful and helpful comments from reviewers of this new edition (in alphabetical order), John Cunningham, Christian Hendershot, Bernard Le Foll, Peter Selby, Wayne Skinner and Tony Toneatto.

Preface to the revised edition

Saying When represents the endpoint of lessons learned from a long program of research on treatment for alcohol use disorders. In the early stages of that research, my dream was to produce a self-help program for people who intend to change their drinking without getting professional help or joining Alcoholics Anonymous or another mutual help group. In my clinical work many clients said that *years* passed between them recognizing the problem and seeking help. Often this delay was because they perceived barriers to entering treatment. The most frequently identified barriers included fear of being defined as "alcoholic," taking time from work or family responsibilities, and lack of services in rural communities. My dream was realized when our research showed that *Saying When*—by itself—yielded outcomes similar to those obtained when therapists dispensed the program.

This new edition continues to include only those components of the program that hundreds of successful clients in our studies consistently used to achieve abstinence or moderate drinking. It was gratifying to learn from reviewing the recent research on self-help programs that *Saying When* remains a state-of-the-art program. This new edition required only small changes. We incorporated recent findings relevant to the guidelines for moderate drinking. Some terms have changed since the last edition so words then in use, such as "alcoholic" or "problem drinker"—which focus on the person—have been replaced in clinical practice by specified levels of "alcohol use disorder"— which focus on the problem.

Repeatedly in my clinical work, clients asked what separates those who succeed with the program from those who do not. The answer from our research is straightforward: those who *persistently* apply the techniques from *Saying When* usually succeed. This is a highly liberating and motivating finding—it means that the key to success is in your hands. You can benefit from the experience of others in terms of what worked for them, and add to it your determination to change.

Saying When offers a well-tested program for those who have good reasons to quit or cut down on their drinking, believe this is the time to make the change, and prefer a self-help guide to attending a clinic. This book is also a useful adjunct for counsellors when helping clients with drinking problems. Now retired from active research and treatment, I find it very rewarding to know that so many people continue to use *Saying When* and benefit from the efforts of my working years.

Foreword

When Dr. Sanchez-Craig began the research that led to *Saying When*, she was decades ahead of developments in the field. Popular belief at the time was that there were only two kinds of people in the world: alcoholics who would be constitutionally incapable of drinking in moderation, and non-alcoholics who could drink with impunity. In other words, there was no one to use a book on moderation: alcoholics couldn't do it, and non-alcoholics didn't need it. It was also widely assumed that people with alcohol problems were incapable of changing on their own without treatment.

Four decades later, her pioneering perspective has become mainstream. Heavy drinking is a health risk for anyone. The forthcoming fifth edition of the *Diagnostic and Statistical Manual* (DSM-V) recognizes that alcohol problems occur all along a continuum of severity. As with chronic medical problems, people benefit from different approaches depending where they are on this continuum. It is now widely recognized that alcohol problems are often resolved without formal treatment. Professional opinion has converged with research findings to agree that moderation is a feasible outcome, though not recommended for those with more severe alcohol dependence. Physicians are encouraged to screen routinely for heavy drinking as a health risk and to advise moderation.

But how should people go about moderating their drinking? *Saying When* offers science-based self-control strategies that have been developed and tested through 40 years of research. There are no unrealistic claims and promises. Instead, this book offers appropriate guidelines for considering whether this is a sensible approach, and a variety of practical strategies to try. In our U.S. studies we found that people working on their own with a self-help book like this were, on average, just as successful in changing their drinking as those working with a counsellor using the same strategies. Canadian studies (including Dr. Sanchez-Craig's own research) have yielded similar findings.

The third edition of *Saying When* continues to make this approach readily available for people who want to cut down (or quit) their drinking. It describes in clear, straightforward language the best-tested self-control methods to avoid risky and problematic alcohol use.

William R. Miller, PhD
Emeritus Distinguished Professor of Psychology and Psychiatry
The University of New Mexico

Introduction

If your drinking is the cause of some of your problems, this guide can help you to quit or cut down. It offers a program that originated at the Addiction Research Foundation in Ontario, Canada, and has been refined and tested for more than 22 years. This self-help book is the final result of this long program of research. It includes techniques that successful clients consistently used to bring their drinking under control. Since its launch, this guide has been used successfully by many hundreds of clients.

The clients who joined the program and contributed to the research were people who sought help because their drinking was a threat to their health, their relationships or their careers. They were highly motivated to change their drinking habits and made this goal a top priority for several months.

Even though drinking was affecting the lives of our clients, they were not "alcoholics"—they had not experienced symptoms of severe alcohol use disorders or problems with other drugs. Also, they were not suffering serious medical or social problems.

The program that helped our clients is outlined in this guide, step by step, so you can apply it to your own situation.

The program can help you if, like our clients:
- you have good reasons for wanting to change your drinking habits
- you make your goal of quitting or cutting down a top priority for several months.

Why offer a guide like this?

There are four good reasons:

1. Many people who develop alcohol problems sort them out on their own, through trial and error. This guide can make it easier for you to quit or cut down by learning about methods that have worked for others.

2. People who overcome drinking problems often cut down rather than quit. Most treatment programs require that you quit drinking entirely. This guide gives you a choice.

3. People often don't know what is meant by "moderate drinking." This guide gives you information on drinking patterns that can help you to avoid alcohol-related problems.

4. Many people who develop alcohol problems don't seek help simply because treatment programs do not provide the options they want to use to deal with their drinking. These are the options our clients wanted:

PRIVACY

They wanted to get help without having to inform their families or employers.

ANONYMITY

They did not want to be labelled "alcoholic" or to openly admit to being "alcoholic."

FLEXIBILITY

They wanted to get help without putting their work or family responsibilities on hold.

CHOICE

They wanted to choose between quitting or cutting down.

This guide gives people a chance to resolve their drinking problems and still retain these important options.

Some people have used this guide as part of a personal wellness program. Their level of drinking was not causing them problems, but they wanted to stay healthy by drinking less, doing more physical exercise or watching their diet.

What has been the success rate of our clients?

During the last 18 years of our research (from 1977 to 1995), we conducted several studies involving clients with mild to moderate alcohol problems. Of the hundreds who took part, about 70 per cent were rated "successful" one to two years after they completed the program. Some clients followed the program with the assistance of a therapist, and others worked on their own using this guide. The rates of success were similar in both groups.

But how did we define success? We considered clients successful if they were "problem-free"—that is, their drinking was no longer causing them the problems that prompted them to seek help (e.g., conflicts with family or friends, missing work, spending too much on alcohol, concerns about their emotional or physical health).

PROFILE OF SUCCESSFUL CLIENTS

When they joined the program, most clients reported drinking daily and frequently consuming five or more drinks on a single occasion. Their weekly average was around 40 drinks. After completing the program, clients who were no longer having problems related to their drinking had adopted a new pattern of drinking that looked like this:

- an average of **3** non-drinking days a week
- an *upper limit* of **4** drinks for men and **3** for women on days when they did drink (they drank at this level only on special occasions; on most days they drank less)
- an *upper limit* of **12** drinks for men and **9** for women in any week.

In earlier versions of this book, we used the above limits in our Guidelines for Moderate Drinking. Recently, new guidelines known as Canada's Low-Risk Alcohol Drinking Guidelines were released (see www.ccsa.ca). Since the daily and weekly limits for drinking in these national guidelines are very similar to those we developed in our research, we decided to use them in *Saying When* to avoid confusion.

How will this guide help you?

Saying When has four main sections.

SECTION 1

This section will help you determine if this guide is for you or if you need more intensive help.

SECTION 2

This section describes the five steps of the program. You will learn the skills that can help you to achieve and maintain abstinence or moderate drinking.

SECTION 3

This section answers five questions our clients often asked: What is alcohol? How much is too much? Is "alcoholism" an inherited disease? How do drinking habits develop? How do people deal with drinking problems? We recommend that you review this section while you complete the steps described in Section 2.

APPENDIX

This section includes materials that will allow you to keep track of your progress. It also includes information on how to find substance use treatment resources in your community, should you decide to seek professional help.

SHOULD YOU USE THIS GUIDE OR SHOULD YOU GET MORE HELP ?

Complete the following assessment questionnaire to determine if:
• you have a severe alcohol use disorder
• you are enduring a personal crisis or have severe ongoing emotional
  distress
• you are having problems with drugs other than alcohol.

If you have any of these problems, this program is NOT for you. You probably need more help than this guide can offer. For information on finding substance use treatment resources in your community, please see page 103.

Do I have a severe alcohol use disorder?

Most people who have a severe alcohol use disorder experience the symptoms described on the next page. Review each point carefully and if the symptom applies to you, check it off ☑.

WITHDRAWAL SYMPTOMS

In the past six months, after I had been drinking, I sometimes experienced:
- ☐ nausea or vomiting
- ☐ the "shakes" (a noticeable tremor in my hands, tongue or eyelids)
- ☐ a lot of sweating
- ☐ panic (strong anxiety)
- ☐ restlessness
- ☐ hallucinations (I saw, heard or felt things that were not really there)
- ☐ headache or feeling that my head was full or tight
- ☐ feeling that I had lost a day or did not know where I was
- ☐ seizures (I lost consciousness and was told that my body was twitching).

DRINKING TO RELIEVE WITHDRAWAL SYMPTOMS

In the past six months, more than once:
- ☐ I needed alcohol to relieve withdrawal symptoms (for instance, I drank in the morning, or when I woke up, to calm the shakes or other unpleasant feelings).
- ☐ I needed alcohol to avoid feeling withdrawal symptoms.

If you checked any of the symptoms described above, you may need more help than this guide can provide. Seek the advice of a health professional.

Do I have other signs of an alcohol use disorder?

If a substance use professional were assessing whether you have an alcohol use disorder, he or she would judge to what degree the following statements were true or not true about you. Read and consider each statement carefully. If the statement, or part of it, is true of you, check it off ☑.

In the past six months:

☐ I often drank larger amounts of alcohol than I intended, or I drank for longer periods than I intended.

☐ I often felt that I should cut down or control my alcohol use, or I made one or more unsuccessful efforts to control it.

☐ I spent a great deal of time trying to get alcohol, drinking alcohol or recovering from the effects of drinking.

☐ I was often intoxicated, or suffering the effects of drinking, during my work, while taking care of my child or during school. Or I put myself and others at risk (for example, by driving under the influence of alcohol).

☐ Because of my drinking, I have given up, or reduced, my involvement in important social, work-related or recreational activities.

☐ I continued to use alcohol in spite of one or more persistent or recurring problems that were being made worse because of my drinking.

☐ My tolerance for alcohol has increased. I need to drink much more to get the effect I want, or I get much less effect if I drink at my previous level.

☐ I have experienced "blackouts," or times when I don't recall what happened when I was drinking.

Our clients usually experienced three, four or even five of these symptoms, but not to an extreme degree—their alcohol use disorder was mild or moderate. They never experienced the severe symptoms described at the top of page 8. If you are not sure about your answers, you may consider:

• consulting a substance use treatment professional to help you with this assessment

• starting this program, but keeping in mind that if you do not make progress, it would be wise to consider more intensive help.

Am I experiencing a personal crisis or severe ongoing emotional distress?

Personal crises and severe ongoing emotional distress make it difficult to change drinking habits without extra help. By crises we mean being in situations that prevent people from functioning *normally* at home or work.

These situations tend to provoke crises:
☐ unstable living arrangements
☐ going through a separation or divorce
☐ being in a child custody dispute
☐ being charged with a serious offence
☐ being unemployed after losing a good job
☐ unstable living arrangements
☐ filing for bankruptcy or having serious financial problems
☐ recent traumas such as physical or sexual abuse
☐ the recent loss of a loved one.

Severe emotional distress may result from a crisis, or it may be ongoing. This may include:
☐ feeling severely depressed or anxious
☐ thinking about harming yourself or others.

If you are experiencing a crisis or ongoing emotional distress, you should seek the advice of a health professional to help you cope with your emotional issues and your drinking.

Once you are feeling better emotionally, if you are still concerned about your drinking, *Saying When* can help you.

Am I having problems with other drugs?

These are some of the drugs that can make a drinking problem even worse:
- tranquillizers (such as Valium, Xanax and Ativan)
- sleeping pills (such as Seconal and Halcion)
- painkillers (such as codeine, Percodan and Demerol)
- marijuana or hashish
- amphetamines or "uppers" (such as crystal meth)
- cocaine.

You have a problem with drugs other than alcohol if one of these statements applies to you:
- I am taking a prescription drug, but not the way my doctor recommended—I usually take more or I take it for conditions other than those for which the medication was prescribed.
- I occasionally use an illegal drug, sometimes with problems and sometimes without problems.
- I frequently use an illegal drug.

If you have any of these problems, this guide is NOT for you. You should seek professional help.

Your decision

☐ **Yes**
I believe this guide can help me. I am motivated to start working on my drinking and to make this goal a top priority. Also, I do not have a severe alcohol use disorder or another problem that requires additional help.

☐ **No**
This guide is not for me. I have a severe alcohol use disorder or another problem that requires additional help.

If you decided that this program is for you, remember that our overall objective is to give you the skills you need to avoid problems related to drinking.

THE PROGRAM

To be successful in this program you must go through the following five steps. You can take each step at your own pace.

STEP 1: TAKING STOCK

First, you will find out how much you are drinking, what situations trigger your drinking, and how alcohol is affecting you. This information will help you set your own benchmark for progress.

STEP 2: SETTING YOUR FIRST GOAL AND DISCOVERING HOW YOU COPE WITH URGES TO DRINK

Whether your goal is abstinence or moderation, for the first two weeks of the program you will be advised to quit drinking. This short period of abstinence will help you to discover how you cope naturally in situations where you experience a strong temptation to drink. Our research shows that those who don't drink during the first two weeks are more successful in achieving their goals.

STEP 3: SETTING YOUR LONG-TERM GOAL

Once you have completed Steps 1 and 2, you will have enough information to help you decide if you want to aim for abstinence or moderation. If you want to learn to moderate your drinking, you will determine how much and how often you will drink, and in what situations you can drink safely.

STEP 4: DEVELOPING STRATEGIES TO REACH ABSTINENCE OR MODERATION

Over a four-week period, you will develop and implement a plan to reach your long-term goal. You will be able to put into practice the strategies our successful clients found most useful in dealing with their drinking.

STEP 5: MAINTAINING YOUR PROGRESS

When you reach Step 5, you will know which strategies work best for you. By applying these strategies consistently, you will reach your goal. By making them "second nature," you will be able to maintain your goal. Remember, success doesn't happen overnight. It may take several weeks or months before you become comfortable with a new pattern of drinking, regardless of whether that means abstinence or moderate drinking.

Your overall objective in this program is to avoid problems from drinking. You can achieve this by quitting altogether or by learning to drink in moderation.

Step 1: Taking stock

This step will help you to determine:
- your current pattern of drinking
- what triggers you to drink too much—we call these your "Activators" of heavy drinking
- the different ways in which alcohol has affected you.

Our clients consistently rated Taking Stock as one of the most important parts of this program. It helped them to look at themselves and discover the nature of their drinking habits, as well as the effect that their drinking was having on their lives. You can complete this step in one sitting.

To take stock you will need:
- the drink chart (shown on the next page), to help you estimate "standard drinks"
- a 12-month calendar
- a pocket calculator, smartphone or pencil and paper.

What is a standard drink?

A standard drink contains a fixed amount of alcohol. This chart shows common alcoholic beverages. For each one, it shows the amount served and alcohol content of one standard drink.

| 341 mL (12 oz.) beer, cider or cooler (5% alcohol) | 142 mL (5 oz.) wine (12% alcohol) | 85 mL (3 oz.) fortified wine (18% alcohol) | 43 mL (1.5 oz.) liquor (40% alcohol) |

Alcohol concentration and size of beverages

The chart above shows the "regular strength" alcohol concentration in each type of beverage. Note, however, that the percentage of alcohol in wines, beers, ciders and coolers varies. Wines can range from 10 to 14 per cent alcohol and beers from less than three to more than seven percent. Note too that home-made wines and beers are not tested for alcohol volume, and often have a higher alcohol concentration than commercial beverages.

The size of container that beverages are sold in also varies—many beers, ciders and coolers are available in "supersize" cans or bottles. Servings of beer and wine sold in bars and restaurants are also often larger than standard drink sizes.

These variations in alcohol concentration and serving size need to be taken into account when estimating standard drinks.

The chart shows some common variations in alcohol concentration, serving, and container size to help you calculate standard drinks.

BEVERAGE	SERVING SIZE	ALCOHOL CONCENTRATION	STANDARD DRINKS
Beer, cider or cooler	341 mL (12 oz.) bottle	7% alcohol	1.4
	473 mL (16 oz.) can	5% alcohol	1.4
	568 mL (20 oz.) pint	5% alcohol	1.6
Wine	170 mL (6 oz.) glass	12% alcohol	1.2
	255 mL (9 oz.) glass	12% alcohol	1.8
	750 mL (26 oz) bottle	12% alcohol	5
Liquor (e.g.,whisky, rum, gin)	375 mL (13 oz) bottle	40% alcohol	9
	750 mL (26 oz) bottle	40% alcohol	18
	1.14 L (40 oz) bottle	40% alcohol	27

Assess your current drinking pattern

Many people underestimate just how much they are really drinking. When our clients began to record their drinking patterns using the method described below, many discovered they were drinking more than they thought.

Take your time, and work carefully. These steps will determine your starting point for the program. You want to make sure you are accurate to obtain the best results.

1. WHAT IS MY USUAL DRINKING STYLE?

Which of the following patterns best describes your drinking style in the last 28 days? (You will use this time period—the last four weeks—to assess your drinking.) Indicate your choice with a check mark ☑.
- ☐ Frequent: I usually drank between four to seven days a week.
- ☐ Weekend: I mostly drank on days off.
- ☐ Binge: I drank heavily for several days and then for several days I abstained or drank very little.
- ☐ Occasional: I drank on three to four days of the four-week period, or less often.

2. MARK "UNUSUAL DAYS"

Examine the previous 28 days of a calendar. Highlight all holidays and special days, including celebrations, parties, business trips and sick days. Include any event that affected your usual drinking pattern. If you have any kind of business or work calendar, it may help you to be more accurate in your assessment of "unusual days."

3. IDENTIFY "NO DRINKING DAYS"

Put a "O" on the days when you had nothing to drink. Were there any days when you usually abstained from drinking?

4. IDENTIFY "DAYS WITH 10 OR MORE DRINKS"

If you drank at this level, identify these days on your calendar and record the number of drinks you had each day. If you don't remember the exact number of drinks on a given day, write a "10." Check your "unusual days" to make sure you don't miss any of these very heavy days.

5. IDENTIFY "DAYS WITH 5–9 DRINKS"

If you drank at this level, identify the days on the calendar and write in the number of drinks you typically drank. Was it 5, 6, 7, 8 or 9 drinks?

6. IDENTIFY "DAYS WITH 1–4 DRINKS"

These are the remaining days in the calendar. Write in the typical number of drinks you had on these days. Was it 1, 2, 3 or 4 drinks?

Don't worry if you haven't been able to remember every drink you had. But keep in mind that most people underestimate their drinking because they forget how many drinks they had on the heavy drinking days (that is, days with five or more drinks).

MY CURRENT DRINKING PATTERN

Now, using the information you have marked on your calendar, you can record your current drinking pattern and calculate your "Weekly Average."

	NUMBER OF DAYS (A)	TYPICAL NUMBER OF DRINKS (B)	TOTALS (A x B)
Days with no drinking	_____		
Days with 1–4 drinks	_____	x _____	= _____
Days with 5–9 drinks	_____	x _____	= _____
Days with 10 or more drinks	_____	x _____	= _____

(= 28 days)   Total drinks (28 days) _____

Weekly Average (total drinks ÷ 4 weeks) _____

If you have trouble filling out the chart, follow these instructions:

1. COLUMN A: NUMBER OF DAYS

Under this column, write in (from your calendar) the number of days you didn't drink any alcohol, had 1–4 drinks, had 5–9 drinks, and had 10 or more drinks. Your answers should add up to 28 to match the 28-day period you are using to record your current drinking pattern.

2. COLUMN B: TYPICAL NUMBER OF DRINKS

Again, using the information from your calendar, write in this column the number of drinks you typically had when you drank 1–4, 5–9, or 10 or more drinks. (As an example, our client Bob wrote "3" in the 1–4 level, "8" in the 5–9 level and "12" in the 10 or more level—see sample chart below.)

3. COLUMN A X B: TOTALS

Multiply column A and column B and write the result for each drinking level. Then, add up the three numbers to get your total drinks in the last 28 days.

4. DIVIDE YOUR TOTAL DRINKS BY 4 TO GET YOUR WEEKLY AVERAGE. PUT THAT NUMBER ON THE CHART.

Is the drinking pattern you just recorded an accurate and valid starting point for this program? Remember, this is the pattern you will be trying to change. Review your numbers to ensure they are accurate.

If the last 28 days do not represent your usual drinking habits, do the exercise again using the four-week period in the past year that best reflects your drinking habits.

SAMPLE CHART

Before you go ahead, look at this chart that was completed by Bob, one of our clients. Use it as a guide, to ensure that your chart has been filled out properly.

	NUMBER OF DAYS (A)		TYPICAL NUMBER OF DRINKS (B)		TOTALS (A x B)
Days with no drinking	4				
Days with 1–4 drinks	9	x	3	=	27
Days with 5–9 drinks	14	x	6	=	84
Days with 10 or more drinks	1	x	10	=	10

(= 28 days)   Total drinks (28 days) 121

Weekly Average (total drinks ÷ 4 weeks) 30

Where do I stand?
DRINKING AMONG ADULTS IN ONTARIO

Compare your Weekly Average to that of people in Ontario. According to a random telephone survey done by the Centre for Addiction and Mental Health in 2009:

21.1%   do not drink
74.0%   have 1–14 drinks
2.5%   have 15–21 drinks
2.4%   have 22 or more drinks

Activators of heavy drinking

This part of Taking Stock will help you to recognize the situations that tend to trigger your heavy drinking. We call these situations the "Activators" of heavy drinking. In Section 3—"Common Questions"—we explain why. It will be useful for you to review the background material in Section 3 before continuing with your assessment.

Knowing your Activators is essential to achieving your goal. Here are the reasons why:

- You will be able to anticipate a situation or a feeling that has caused you to drink too much—for instance, feeling lonely on the weekend. Then you can make plans to keep busy and avoid drinking at all or drinking too much.
- You can figure out ways to stay within your limits in situations where alcohol is available—for instance at parties, at a bar with friends or during business trips.
- You can decide to avoid situations where you know you will be tempted to drink too much. You can avoid going to events where the pressure to drink is likely to be strong.

The Activators listed on the following pages are those our clients identified most often. These Activators fall into three main categories.

They trigger:
1. drinking to cope (with negative feelings and to make things easier)
2. drinking for pleasure
3. drinking out of habit.

You may find this exercise challenging. Be patient and persistent. You will give yourself a very important tool for your success!

MY ACTIVATORS OF HEAVY DRINKING

Below is the list of situations or circumstances that our clients told us encouraged them to drink more than they wanted.

Review the list carefully and check ☑ only those situations in which you had too much to drink in the past year, even if it only happened once. For the purpose of this task, "too much" means whatever you believe is too much for you.

I DRANK TO COPE WITH NEGATIVE FEELINGS

☐ When I felt generally low or depressed
☐ When I was angry at myself or someone else
☐ When I was bored
☐ When I was anxious about something
☐ When I was sad and feeling sorry for myself
☐ When I was frustrated because things did not go my way
☐ When I felt guilty about what I had done or not done
☐ When I felt stressed or tired
☐ When I felt rejected by someone I cared about
☐ When I was criticized by my family, friends or boss
☐ When I felt lonely
☐ Any other negative feelings _____

I DRANK TO MAKE THINGS EASIER FOR MYSELF

☐ To help me release anger or frustration
☐ To help me socialize more comfortably
☐ To help me talk to strangers
☐ To help me have sex
☐ To help me express affection or other emotions
☐ To help me speak up for myself or stand up for myself to others
☐ To help me get through boring chores or tasks
☐ To help me get to sleep
☐ To help me forget about physical pain
☐ To help me get rid of a hangover
☐ To help me do anything else _____

TIMES WHEN I DRANK TOO MUCH FOR PLEASURE

☐ To enjoy the "buzz" or sensation of feeling "high"
☐ To catch up to the "high" of friends
☐ At parties
☐ To enjoy the taste of the drinks
☐ During special celebrations like weddings or birthdays
☐ To enjoy family reunions
☐ With meals
☐ When something good happened that made me feel like celebrating
☐ After I did physical exercise
☐ When enjoying leisure activities such as fishing or playing cards
☐ When visiting friends or having company at home
☐ While on holidays
☐ To reward myself for achieving success or working hard
☐ Any other drinking for pleasure _____

TIMES WHEN I DRANK TOO MUCH OUT OF HABIT

☐ As soon as I arrived home from work
☐ With a particular person or group of people
☐ After work or school with the same people
☐ While doing my chores, or at work

☐ When watching television
☐ When alcohol was available
☐ With meals (lunch, dinner)
☐ Whenever certain people invited me for a drink
☐ Whenever I was offered a drink
☐ Any other habitual drinking _____

Now take a good look at the situations you marked. These situations put you at risk of drinking too much. From now on, you will need to be careful in these situations. To help reach your goal, you will need to develop ways to avoid drinking or heavy drinking in these situations.

Be aware that less frequent events such as a vacation, a business trip or a conference can also present a serious risk to you.

Assess how alcohol has affected you

Our clients told us that the physical symptoms and problems caused by their drinking motivated them to change their drinking habits. Once they managed to get their drinking under control, their health and quality of life improved.

MY PHYSICAL SYMPTOMS—IN THE PAST YEAR

These are symptoms you experienced while you were drinking, or immediately after an episode of heavy drinking. Review the list and check the answer that best describes your situation:

• Frequently—I experienced the symptom almost every week.
• Occasionally—I experienced the symptom once or twice a month or less often.
• Never—I did not experience the symptom.

	FREQUENTLY	OCCASIONALLY	NEVER
Difficulty in getting to sleep	☐	☐	☐
Waking during the night	☐	☐	☐
Headache or hangover	☐	☐	☐
Nausea, room spinning, vomiting	☐	☐	☐
Stomach cramps, diarrhea	☐	☐	☐
Rapid heartbeat	☐	☐	☐
Shakiness, unsteady hands	☐	☐	☐
Sweating, particularly at night	☐	☐	☐
Poor memory (can't remember things)	☐	☐	☐
Difficulty concentrating	☐	☐	☐
Mood or personality changes (irritable, more sociable)	☐	☐	☐
Feeling sluggish, without energy	☐	☐	☐

If you have been experiencing any of these symptoms, you will find they will begin to disappear—either immediately or after a few days—as you cut down or abstain.

MY PROBLEMS—IN THE PAST YEAR

When our clients stopped drinking or cut down to moderate levels, they usually reported feeling healthier and happier with themselves. Their relationships at home and work tended to improve dramatically.

If you have already gone through a broken marriage or job loss because of your drinking, cutting back or quitting can't undo the damage. But it can help you to prevent these problems from happening again.

How has your drinking affected you in the past year? Here is a list of areas that may have been affected. In the space provided, write examples that apply in your situation.

Physical health (e.g., illness or accidents): _____
_____
_____
_____

Emotional health (e.g., felt depressed, disgusted with myself): _____
_____
_____
_____

Job performance (e.g., missing work, lower performance, complaints from supervisor, co-workers, union representatives): _____
_____
_____
_____

Important relationships (e.g., complaints from family, disputes with family or friends about drinking): _____
_____
_____
_____

Leisure/free-time activities (e.g., reduced or neglected physical exercise, hobbies or other pastimes): _____
_____
_____
_____

Financial issues (e.g., spending too much money on alcohol—most of our clients were shocked to find they spent up to thousands of dollars a year): _____

_____

_____

_____

Legal issues (e.g., driving while impaired, whether charged or not; assault, whether charged or not): _____

_____

_____

_____

Confirm your commitment

Now that you have taken stock, review these questions carefully:

Is my drinking putting my health at risk? If so, how? _____

_____

_____

_____

Why should I change my drinking habits now? (List your reasons. If you are unsure, review your answers in "My physical symptoms" and "My problems" on pages 24 to 27.) _____

_____

_____

_____

What other priorities do I have that might interfere with my determination to change my drinking habits? _____

_____

_____

_____

How am I going to keep my goal of quitting or cutting down as one of the most important things I do over the next few months?_____

_____

_____

_____

Am I going to use this guide, or will I find another way to deal with my drinking? _____

_____

_____

_____

Step 2: Setting your first goal and discovering how you cope with urges to drink

This step will help you to:
• set your first goal
• identify strategies to help you to achieve that goal
• identify how you cope with urges to drink
• assess your progress after two weeks in the program.

Most people take about two weeks to complete this step. Think of these two weeks as a period of rapid adjustment. This is usually the period of most dramatic change in the program. Hard work here prepares you for success in the long run.

Ways to quit drinking or cut back

There are different ways to quit drinking or cut down to moderate levels. If you are not yet sure of your final drinking goal, don't worry. The first two weeks of the program will help you to make the right choice. Don't rush into making a decision—it's too important.

Here are the different ways you can quit or cut down:
• You can cut down gradually until you successfully reach abstinence or a level of moderate drinking.

- You can start drinking moderately or quit drinking altogether from day one of the program, and stick to your decision for good.
- You can abstain from drinking for the first two weeks of the program and then decide whether you want to continue to abstain or drink moderately.

We urged our clients to stop drinking for the first two weeks of the program for several reasons. Two weeks of abstinence are likely to:

- **Increase your chance of success.** Clients who abstain during the first two weeks of the program are usually more successful in reaching their long-term goals.
- **Improve your health.** Clients who abstain for the first two weeks report feeling healthier and more energetic, and say they sleep better.
- **Improve your mental abilities**. Frequent heavy drinking dulls your ability to think, but your mental abilities will sharpen quickly after two weeks of abstinence. It is important to be clear-headed when you are learning a new pattern of behaviour.
- **Reduce your tolerance for alcohol.** Clients who stopped drinking for two weeks at the beginning of the program (and who later successfully reached a goal of moderation) often told us that they felt a stronger effect from two to three drinks when they resumed drinking than they had before the period of abstinence. Having a lower tolerance to the effects of alcohol can make it easier to drink less.
- **Help you to identify your best coping skills.** If you abstain, you are likely to experience urges to drink. Dealing with these urges will help you to discover situations where you are at risk of drinking too much and your best ways of coping.

Should I be concerned about abstaining for the first two weeks?

About 50 per cent of our clients were able to abstain completely for the first two weeks. Those who continued to drink did so because they had:

- **Special events**. Some clients had birthdays, weddings or other special events coming up at which they wanted to have one or two drinks to celebrate.
- **Concerns about failing**. Some clients believed they could only achieve their goal if they took it step by step. They were afraid of failing if their goal seemed too ambitious. They preferred to cut down gradually.
- **Concerns about withdrawal symptoms**. Other clients preferred to cut down gradually because they didn't want the discomfort of withdrawal symptoms. Usually these clients had been drinking 10 or more drinks every day for at least the last three months. People with an "early" alcohol problem usually don't drink at this level.

Even if you have not been drinking heavily, you may still experience some mild withdrawal symptoms if you abstain or cut down sharply. These include anxiety, shaky hands, sweating or difficulty sleeping. These symptoms can be uncomfortable, but they don't last very long and are no worse than having the flu.

To help you through this period, it's best if you remain quiet and calm, and have emotional support from a friend or family member. Remember, this is one situation in which the "short-term pain" really gives you "long-term gain."

If you experience severe withdrawal symptoms, go to the emergency department of the nearest general hospital. These symptoms include:
- strong shakes—you can't hold a full cup without spilling the contents
- excessive sweating and feeling very hot
- wanting to vomit after each meal
- lack of appetite and fear of eating
- mental confusion—for example, losing track of time and not knowing where you are
- hallucinations—hearing, seeing or feeling things that aren't there.
- seizures—losing consciousness and being told by others that your body was twitching.

Remember, this program is not for people with severe alcohol problems. If you have a severe alcohol use disorder, the best thing you can do is to seek professional assessment and advice. If you have a severe alcohol use disorder, do not stop drinking suddenly if you have ever had a seizure or if you are pregnant. Please see the treatment resources listed on page 103.

Setting your first goal

During the next two weeks, I plan to:
☐ A) Abstain completely from alcohol.
☐ B) Cut down gradually, reducing the amount I drink, or the frequency, or both.
☐ C) Abstain, except at one or two special events where I will drink one or two drinks. These are the events I plan to attend: _____
_____
_____

If you choose option (B) or option (C), fill in the blanks below with what you consider realistic limits for your alcohol consumption. If you choose to abstain completely, fill in the blanks with "O."

	WEEK 1	WEEK 2
Maximum number of days I will drink	____ days	____ days
Maximum number of drinks I will have on any day	____ drinks	____ drinks
Maximum number of drinks I will have each week	____ drinks	____ drinks

Am I confident I can achieve this goal?

If you are fairly confident about achieving your goal, go ahead and try it.

If your confidence is low, rethink the goal and make the limits more realistic. For instance, if you are thinking about abstaining but find that two weeks is too long, make a commitment to abstain for one week. When the week is over, you can then decide about the second week.

If you choose to gradually cut back on your drinking, make sure that the goals you set are realistic but challenging. For instance, in the first week you may lower your daily amount by two or three drinks. In the second week, you could further decrease the number of drinks you have and increase the days of abstinence.

Strategies to achieve your first goal

KEEP TRACK OF YOUR DRINKING

Our clients consistently rated this strategy as one of the most important to their progress. Keep a daily record of the days when you drink and when you don't. This diary will give you:
• a greater sense of self-control
• a better understanding of situations in which you are tempted to drink over your limit
• a sense of accomplishment and pride when you can look back on a good record over past weeks and months.

Use the Drinking Diary in the Appendix (page 89) to make your records. This strategy is an essential part of this program.

PICK STRATEGIES THAT WILL WORK FOR YOU

Here are some strategies our clients found useful when they were trying to achieve their first goal. If you have tried to reduce your drinking in the past, it is likely you have already used some of these strategies, and some may have been helpful. Go through the list and check ☑ those you believe will make it easier to achieve your first goal. Make a note of other strategies that have helped before or seem promising now.

- ☐ Do not buy alcohol in the next two weeks.
- ☐ Do not keep alcohol at home or within sight.
- ☐ Stock up on your favorite non-alcoholic drinks.
- ☐ Avoid contact with heavy-drinking friends.
- ☐ Seek support from family or friends.
- ☐ Do something else with your time instead of drinking. Find some fun activities you've always wanted to try or do something that gives you a sense of accomplishment.
- ☐ Decide which situations you should avoid.
- ☐ Remind yourself often of why you want to change your drinking habits and how it will improve your life when you succeed.

Make a note of promising strategies _____
_____
_____
_____
_____

KEEP TRACK OF HOW YOU COPE WITH URGES TO DRINK

Whether you decided to abstain for the next two weeks, or to cut down on your drinking, you will probably be tempted to drink above the limits you set.

Urges to drink are triggered by your Activators—the things that make you feel like drinking—and are most likely to happen in situations in which you drank in the past.

Keeping track of these situations can help you in two important ways:
• You can gain greater understanding of your Activators.

- You can discover how you cope naturally with urges to drink above your limit. This will allow you to achieve your long-term goal more quickly and with less effort.

Use the Coping Diary in the Appendix (page 95) to keep a record of how you cope with clear temptations to exceed your goal.

Coping effectively with urges to drink is a challenge, especially when you are just beginning to break the habit. But remember, each time you cope successfully with an urge you are weakening your drinking habit and getting closer to your goal.

Examples of coping with urges to drink

The following examples show how to record the relevant information in your Coping Diary. Keep in mind that the best coping responses are those that are simple and direct.

Bob watched a hockey game at Sam's house. He was determined to abstain for the week. But when Sam offered him a beer, he was tempted. Bob found himself struggling with a decision.

DESCRIPTION DE MON ENVIE DE BOIRE	
Heure _21 h30_ Lieu _chez un ami_ J'étais avec _Pierre et George_	
Mes sentiments _agité et frustré_	
CE QUE J'AI FAIT	
Je me suis dit _je me suis promis que je ne boivais pas cette semaine_	
Voici ce que j'ai fait pour résister à l'envie de boire _j'ai demandé une boisson gazeuse à Pierre_	
Quand on m'a offert de l'alcool, j'ai refusé en disant _je ne bois pas aujourd'hui_	
MA MÉTHODE A-T-ELLE ÉTÉ EFFICACE ? ☒ Oui ☐ Non	

JOURNAL DE BORD : COMMENT JE FAIT FACE AUX ENVIES DE BOIRE

Mary was criticized by her boss at the end of the day. She was upset because she was not given the opportunity to tell her side of what happened. When she got home, she recalled the incident. She became angry and was tempted to have a drink to cope with her feelings.

DETAILS OF MY URGE TO DRINK

Time of day __7:30 pm__ Place __home__ I was with __alone__

My feelings __angry & frustrated__

HOW I HANDLED IT

This is what I said to myself __I shouldn't let these feelings throw me off base. drinking won't help__

This is what I did to cope __I wrote a list of counter arguments & called a friend for advice__

This is how I said 'no' when I was invited to drink _____

DID MY COPING STRATEGY WORK? ☒ Yes ☐ No

COPING DIARY

Tom decided to have no more than two drinks at the party. He watched himself carefully, and by the end of the evening he had reached his limit. Shortly after, Tom and other friends "caught their second wind" and started to party all over again. Everyone was drinking and Tom felt a strong urge to have another drink and join in the fun.

DETAILS OF MY URGE TO DRINK

Time of day __12:30 am__ Place __friend's__ I was with __group of friends__

My feelings __energetic. in a party mood__

HOW I HANDLED IT

This is what I said to myself __I've been good all night. I can handle one more drink__

This is what I did to cope __nothing. I ended up having too many__

This is how I said 'no' when I was invited to drink __nothing. I just took the drink__

DID MY COPING STRATEGY WORK? ☒ Yes ☐ No

COPING DIARY

Jane was trying to break her habit of drinking before dinner. She got home from a rough day at work after being stuck in traffic for almost two hours. She found herself thinking about having a drink to relax and unwind.

DETAILS OF MY URGE TO DRINK

Time of day _7:00 pm_ Place _home_ I was with _alone_

My feelings _frustrated & tense_

HOW I HANDLED IT

This is what I said to myself _do I really need a drink to unwind?_

This is what I did to cope _went for a brisk walk_

This is how I said 'no' when I was invited to drink _____

DID MY COPING STRATEGY WORK? ☒ Yes ☐ No

COPING DIARY

I have discovered I can say "NO" to urges to drink!

Keep track of the effective ways you have found to cope with an urge to drink over your set limit.

These were the best ways of saying "NO" to myself when I had the urge to drink over my goal: _____

These were my best ways of saying "NO" to others when they invited me to drink: _____

These were things I did to help me avoid drinking or heavy drinking: _____

EVALUATE YOUR PROGRESS AFTER ABOUT TWO WEEKS

If you have been abstinent for the past two weeks, or have cut down a lot, you are probably ready to decide about your long-term goal. Proceed to Step 3.

However, if by the end of the second or third week you have not been able to cut back your drinking significantly, there are three probable explanations:

1. You may not be fully determined to change your drinking habits. Reconsider your reasons. Look again at the section on Taking Stock (Step 1).

2. You may not have put enough time and effort into achieving your goal. Think again about the priority you are willing to give to changing your drinking. Did you work at it every day?

3. Your drinking problem may be more severe than you thought.

If you think your problem is more severe than you had anticipated, you may need more help than this program can offer. We advise you to seek professional help. See page 103 for information on finding treatment resources in your community.

Step 3: Setting your long-term goal

This step will help you to:
• choose your long-term goal and the best way to achieve it
• specify your limits for drinking (if you choose moderation), using the guidelines for "moderate drinking."

Remember, the overall objective of this program is to help you avoid problems from drinking. You can achieve this goal by abstaining altogether or by learning to drink in moderation.

Pros and cons of abstinence and moderation

Doing this exercise can give you a sense of why some people favour abstinence and some people prefer to cut down. You probably have your own list of pros and cons. Consider them as well.

Abstinence

PROS	CONS
• is likely to be supported by family or friends who were hurt by your drinking	• may mean "standing out" in a group of people who drink
• makes sense if your main reason for drinking was to get intoxicated	• may be seen by others as indicating "poor control" over drinking
• saves you the cost of alcoholic beverages	• restricts your range of beverages
• means you avoid risks from drinking	

Moderation

PROS	CONS
• may make it easier to "fit in" with people who drink socially	• isn't risk-free—drinking at any level carries some risk
• indicates self-control over drinking	• means measuring, counting, recording drinks
• means you can still enjoy drinks	• may make friends or family concerned because of past problems

Before you make your long-term choice, think about the pros and cons of each goal and review the guidelines for moderate drinking below. Make a note about any other factors you think apply to your situation.

Notes: _____

_____

_____

_____

_____

_____

What is moderate drinking?

Drinking in moderation means consuming alcohol in ways that do not interfere with your responsibilities at home, work or school, or your important relationships; and that minimize the risk of serious illnesses and harms to yourself and others (e.g., injury). To set goals of moderation we use the levels of drinking suggested in Canada's Low-Risk Alcohol Drinking Guidelines,* issued in 2012, as outlined below:

- Plan non-drinking days every week. Successful clients typically abstained **3** days per week. This helped them to break the habit.
- Set limits to reduce your long-term health risks: Women no more than **10** drinks a week, with no more than **2** drinks a day most days; men no more than **15** drinks a week, with no more than **3** drinks a day most days.
- Set limits to reduce your risk of injury and harm: No more than **3** drinks for women and **4** drinks for men on a single occasion.
- Avoid intoxication: Don't drink more than **1** drink per hour or more than **2** drinks in any three-hour period.
- Never drink to cope (e.g., to feel less bored or anxious, to give yourself courage to act).
- Don't make alcohol an important part of your recreational activities.
- Never drink during or before risky activities (e.g., driving, boating, swimming or operating machinery).

Important notes:
The daily and weekly limits recommended here are **upper limits—not targets**. All drinking has risks; the lower your drinking, the lower the risks.

Sometimes it is best not to drink at all. For instance, if you are pregnant, planning to become pregnant or are about to breastfeed; if you take medications that interact with alcohol or have a health problem

* It is interesting to note that the limits for alcohol use recommended in the new national guidelines, which are based on studies of health and disease of populations, are similar to the limits we recommended in 1987, based on reports of our successful clients (see page 3). To learn more about Canada's Low-Risk Alcohol Drinking Guidelines, visit www.ccsa.ca.

that could be worsened by drinking; if you are responsible for the safety of others or need to make important decisions; if you are younger than the legal drinking age.

Consult a physician if you are concerned about the effects of alcohol use on your physical or mental health.

Setting your long-term goal

If you were successful in abstaining for the first two weeks, or you achieved your goals of reducing your drinking, you are probably ready to set your long-term goal. Remember, the decision you make now is not carved in stone. As you progress, you may decide to change or adjust your goal. However, any changes should be made only after careful thought—not on the spur of the moment.

Check your option:
☐ Abstinence
If you chose to stop drinking altogether and you are no longer drinking, proceed to Steps 4 and 5. *Saying When* will show you ways to help you maintain your abstinence.

☐ Moderation
If you chose to drink moderately and did not abstain during the first two weeks, but you have been cutting down, you may want to reduce your drinking even more before you set your long-term goal. If you abstained, or feel ready to specify your goal, do it now.

It is best if you stay within the moderate drinking levels as explained on page 41. Specify your goal in the following ways:

Maximum number of drinks I will have on any day   _____ drinks

Maximum number of days I will drink in any week   _____ days

Maximum number of drinks I will have each week _____ drinks

Beverages I will drink _____

RISKY SITUATIONS

What are the situations in which I may be tempted to go over my set limits? (Review your Activators and remember that any kind of drinking to cope is risky.) _____

_____

_____

_____

OK SITUATIONS

What are the situations in which I know I could drink for pleasure, to enjoy the taste, to enhance meals or just to socialize? (Make sure that these are situations in which you can manage your drinking without getting carried away.) _____

_____

_____

_____

I will assess whether this goal suits my lifestyle for _____ weeks.

CHECK YOUR CONFIDENCE

Are you confident you will be able to stay within the limits of your goal? If you are not sure you can meet your goal, adjust it to a level you feel more comfortable with.

Learning to drink moderately in a way that suits your lifestyle may take time and some experimentation. Keep adjusting your goal to minimize the risk of problems. Remember, moderation means a good blend of days when you abstain, and days when you drink within the guidelines.

EXAMPLES OF SETTING LONG-TERM GOALS

The following are examples of goals that successful clients adopted.

Regular moderate drinking

Maximum number of drinks I will have on any day ___3___

Maximum number of days I will drink in any week ___4___ days

Maximum number of drinks I will have each week ___10___ drinks

RISKY SITUATIONS

To cope with boredom

To please friends at parties

To help me sleep

OK SITUATIONS

With special meals

When Socializing

Regular light drinking

Maximum number of drinks I will have on any day ___2___

Maximum number of days I will drink in any week ___5___ days

Maximum number of drinks I will have each week ___9___ drinks

RISKY SITUATIONS

To cope with frustrations

To unwind from work

To feel more at ease with people

OK SITUATIONS

With meals

When visiting friends

Occasional light drinking

Maximum number of drinks I will have on any day   2

Maximum number of days I will drink in any week   2   days

Maximum number of drinks I will have each week   3   drinks

RISKY SITUATIONS

To assert myself with people

To get high

When I'm alone

OK SITUATIONS

Special celebrations

Special outings

Step 4: Developing strategies to reach abstinence or moderation

Consider the five strategies our clients find most useful in dealing with their drinking. These strategies can help you achieve your goal:
• Keep track of your drinking.
• Pace your drinking.
• Plan ahead to avoid heavy drinking.
• Develop leisure and other free-time activities.
• Find ways to cope with problems without drinking.

Clients who used these strategies regularly were more successful than those who used them only occasionally. You can develop your own effective program based on these five strategies over the next four to six weeks. During this time, you will find out which strategies suit you and can help you maintain your progress over the long term.

Keeping track of your drinking

As we've said, keeping a daily record of your drinking and days of abstinence is the strategy our clients rated as "most helpful."

Our research showed that clients who recorded their drinking every day for at least three months were more successful in reaching and maintaining their goal than clients who kept records only briefly.

In Step 2, you learned how to use the Drinking Diary. Please remember to update your records every day. If you leave it to memory, your records will be less accurate.

Keeping a daily record of your drinking and non-drinking days keeps you focused on your goal and increases your chances of reaching that goal.

EXAMPLE

These records belong to a client who abstained for the first two weeks of the program. He then chose a goal of moderation. According to his records, in Week 3 he exceeded his maximum quantity by two drinks on Saturday, and his weekly goal by one drink. In Week 4, he drank on one day more than he had intended. Feedback from these records helped him to stay on track over the following weeks.

JOURNAL DE BORD : MA CONSOMMATION D'ALCOOL	MON OBJECTIF POUR LA SEMAINE	3	N^{bre} maximum de verres par jour __3__ / N^{bre} maximum de jours de consommation cette semaine __3__ / N^{bre} maximum de verres d'alcool cette semaine __9__							
				L	M	M	J	V	S	D	
	# OF 12 OZ BOTTLES BEER			0	2	0	1	0	2	0	TOTAL # OF DRINKS THIS WEEK ▼
	# OF 5 OZ GLASSES WINE			0	0	0	2	0	2	0	
	# OF 3 OZ GLASSES FORT WINE*			0	0	0	0	0	1	0	
	# OF 1½ OZ SHOTS LIQUOR			0	0	0	0	0	0	0	
	TOTAL DRINKS PER DAY			0	2	0	3	0	5	0	10

* VIN FORTIFIÉ (p. ex., xérès, porto, vermouth)

DRINKING DIARY	MY GOAL FOR WEEK #	4	MAX # OF DRINKS PER DAY __3__ / MAX # OF DRINKING DAYS THIS WEEK __3__ / MAX # OF DRINKS THIS WEEK __9__							
			M	T	W	T	F	S	S	
	# OF 12 OZ BOTTLES BEER		0	0	2	1	0	1	2	TOTAL # OF DRINKS THIS WEEK ▼
	# OF 5 OZ GLASSES WINE		0	0	0	1	0	2	0	
	# OF 3 OZ GLASSES FORT WINE*		0	0	0	0	0	0	0	
	# OF 1½ OZ SHOTS LIQUOR		0	0	0	0	0	0	0	
	TOTAL DRINKS PER DAY		0	0	2	2	0	3	2	9

* FORT WINE (e.g., sherry, port, vermouth)

Pacing your drinking—a must if your goal is moderation

This means being aware of how much and how quickly you are drinking. If you start to feel a "buzz," be on guard, because the normal tendency is to relax and begin to ignore your goal.

Practise these strategies to help you "keep your wits about you" when you drink:
- Measure all of your drinks.
- Dilute your drinks (to lower the concentration of alcohol). Some people use half a drink at a time, well-diluted (for instance, a "spritzer"). This should help you to drink more slowly.
- Sip your drinks—don't gulp.
- Allow at least one hour between drinks.
- Alternate alcoholic and non-alcoholic beverages.
- Avoid drinking without having some food.
- Avoid cocktails that contain more than one standard drink.

Another successful moderate drinking strategy you may want to adopt is to switch to beverages with lower alcohol concentrations, such as light beer or light wine. Here are some examples of how much less you would be drinking:
- Light beer (3 to 4 per cent alcohol) has 20 percent less alcohol than regular beer.
- Light wine (7 per cent) has 40 percent less alcohol than regular 12 per cent wine.
- A mixed drink made with a one-ounce instead of a one-and-a-half-ounce shot of liquor has 33 per cent less alcohol than a standard drink.

MY PACING STRATEGIES

These are strategies I plan to use to pace my drinking: _____
_____
_____
_____

Planning ahead to avoid heavy drinking

In situations where alcohol is readily available, many people find it tough to stick to their intended limit. This is also true in situations where they are pressured to drink.

When you are beginning to abstain or to drink in moderation, you need to plan in advance how you are going to deal with the pressure in social situations. Plan to protect yourself before you attend.

Before going to a social event, you should always:
• decide whether you will drink at all
• plan effective ways of saying "NO" to yourself and "NO" to others— you may want to use different approaches, one for people you know and another for those you have just met.

Other strategies you may consider:
• Ask someone you trust to help you stay on target. He or she may help you by giving you "half" drinks or non-alcoholic drinks, or by reminding you of your limit.
• Find a simple way to keep an accurate count of the drinks you consume. One way is to move a coin from one pocket to another for each drink; another is to keep the bottle caps for each drink in your pocket.
• Be ready to use a good excuse to get you off the hook. For instance, "No thanks, I'm driving" or "I'm not drinking tonight."

Learn to say "NO" to people who invite you to have a drink. It can be tough, especially when they insist. But you can say "NO." Be persistent, but polite.

SITUATIONS IN WHICH I NEED TO PLAN AHEAD

Record situations that put you at risk of drinking too much. Write down how you plan to stay within your limit.

Situation A: _____

My plan: _____

_____

_____

_____

Situation B: _____

My plan: _____

_____

_____

_____

Situation C: _____

My plan: _____

_____

_____

_____

Situation D: _____

My plan: _____

_____

_____

_____

EXAMPLES

Consider how our clients Lynn and Ron prepared themselves for situations in which they previously had too much to drink.

Lynn decided to go to the company party. She knew that an alcoholic punch would be served along with other beverages. She also knew co-workers who sometimes drank too much would probably pressure her to drink. At previous company parties, Lynn had made a fool of herself by drinking too much. She decided she wouldn't let it happen again.

Situation: _Company party_

Lynn's plan: _Avoid the punch...only drink what I can measure. Have soft drinks till I get a feel for the party. Stay no more than 3 hours. If offered a drink, ask for tonic. Have boyfriend pick me up._

Lynn left the party as planned, feeling proud of herself.

Ron had to travel almost every week on business, often overseas. He was at risk of drinking heavily when he travelled alone. Usually he would start drinking before departure at the airport, and would continue during the flight and upon arrival at his hotel room.

Situation: _Business trip_

Ron's plan: _Make business calls from airport lounge. Only drink juice on the plane. Bring clothes to work out in or swim at the hotel._

After this plan was put into action, Ron found that his business trips cost less and were more productive.

Developing leisure and other free-time activities

Clients who successfully learned to abstain or to moderate their drinking made a deliberate effort to replace the hours they spent drinking with other activities. Unsuccessful clients often failed to fill the time they spent drinking with activities they enjoyed or that gave them a sense of satisfaction. See "My leisure and free-time activities," below.

What are some alternative activities to drinking?
• Do things that give you pleasure. You may like to go to movies, exercise, play a sport or make crafts. You can visit friends who do not encourage heavy drinking.
• Do things that give you a sense of accomplishment and pride. You may like to help your children with their homework, do volunteer work, catch up with household chores, go shopping or do some gardening.

Often the things that give a sense of accomplishment also give you a sense of pleasure.

MY LEISURE AND FREE-TIME ACTIVITIES

Record activities you think you would enjoy doing consistently during time you usually spent drinking. Make a complete list and think about the leisure time you have during work days and non-work days.

_____

_____

_____

_____

Overcoming a habit of heavy drinking may require major changes in your lifestyle. If you have difficulty developing enjoyable activities to replace your drinking hours, get help from a qualified counsellor.

EXAMPLES

Joe broke the habit of having a drink as soon as he arrived home from work by:
- taking his dog for a walk
- spending time with his kids, or
- helping with dinner.

He also thought he would have time to do woodwork in his workshop, but he found that by the time he changed his clothes and got set up, he would only have 10 or 15 minutes before dinner was ready.

Kate used to drink at home by herself, usually on Friday nights and on Saturdays starting at noon. Mostly, she drank out of boredom—even though she could have called up friends to go out. To break the habit of drinking on weekends, this is what Kate decided:
- She would call a friend early in the week to arrange a date for dinner or a movie.
- If nobody was available, she would go shopping on her own.
- On Saturdays she would visit her parents, or take tennis lessons at the local community centre.

In the past, Kate had enjoyed skiing. She decided to join a fitness club, using the money she had saved by not drinking. That way, she could get herself in shape to hit the ski slopes again.

Coping with problems without drinking

Problems of daily life can upset your plan to abstain or drink moderately. These problems can range from minor irritations, such as missing the bus, to personal catastrophes, such as the death of a loved one, a serious illness, a divorce or the loss of your job. Our clients often found that problems that threatened their progress involved:
- ongoing conflicts with another person, and
- experiencing negative feelings.

Because you cannot predict the specific problems you will have, or when they will occur, it is wise to have a strategy to tackle each problem as it comes along.

The problem-solving strategy in this guide will help you to develop two basic ways of coping—coping by acting and coping by thinking. This is how each one works:

Coping by acting can help you change a bad situation into a better one. Coping by acting is very useful when you have problems with other people. By changing your usual approach, you can make the other person react more positively.

Coping by thinking can help you make painful situations more tolerable. This way of coping is especially useful when there is little or nothing you can do to change a situation (for example, the death of a loved one). Although you cannot change these situations directly, you can always change the way you think about them.

Coping by thinking does not mean "fooling yourself" or denying that a situation is serious or dangerous. It means studying the situation from different angles to check (1) if the way you think about it is accurate and (2) if your feelings are a natural reaction to the situation, or if you are over-reacting.

No one likes to experience negative feelings, but often they follow naturally from things that happen to us. It's normal to grieve when a loved one dies, or feel angry or frustrated after being laid off from work. Sometimes, however, we get really upset about things and blow them out of proportion. Whether or not the emotional reaction is valid, drinking to cope with problems is never effective in the long run.

General problem-solving strategy

This strategy offers a method to approach problems of daily life in a systematic way. These are the four steps:

1. **Identify the problem.** Try to recognize the key elements of the situation that troubles you. Ask yourself:
   - What exactly troubles me?
   - What are my feelings about the situation?
   - What are my thoughts about the situation?
   - How do I usually handle it?
   - What are the consequences of my actions?

2. **Consider new approaches.** Think of other ways to handle the situation. At this point, don't worry about how sensible or practical they are, but consider:
   - *New ways of thinking.* What you think affects what you do. When you are upset, your thinking may be rigid, negative and self-defeating. This kind of thinking usually leads to ineffective coping. Consider different ways of looking at the situation. Usually there is more than one reasonable way of thinking about the same situation.
   - *New ways of acting.* In order to turn a bad situation into a good one, it is important to put your usual approach on hold and try new approaches. Find as many options as you can, even if at first glance they seem unrealistic.

3. **Select the most promising approach.** After you have thought of the different options to solve a problem, select the most promising one. Think about how you would use this approach and how effective it would be. Ask yourself:
   - Is this approach going to have positive results? If so, why?
   - Is the approach practical and realistic?

4. **Assess whether your new approach worked.** Before you try your new approach, rehearse it in your mind. Imagine yourself in the situation.

If possible, act it out in private. Then try it out at the appropriate time. To assess whether your approach worked, ask yourself:
- Did I get the positive results I wanted?
- Could I have done something else to make my approach more effective?

If your approach did not work, or you were unable to put it into practice, don't give up. Try another one. There is always more than one solution to a problem.

The following examples illustrate the use of this problem-solving strategy.

Example 1: Marital conflict

Our client was a 30-year-old computer expert who came to the program because his drinking was interfering with his work. He had been married three years. Shortly after his marriage, he and his wife had agreed to open a combined savings account for the purchase of a house.

Identifying the problem: The client's wife was giving lump sums of money to her sister from their joint savings account, without first consulting him. When he found out he felt very angry, and thought she had no right to take money from their joint account to help her sister without discussing it openly with him. To cope with his anger, he started drinking. After three or four drinks he would become verbally abusive, and drink until he was drunk. Then his wife wouldn't talk to him for several days. He felt guilty.

Considering new approaches: When we asked, "Are there any other ways in which you can think about your wife's behaviour?" he said, "Probably she goes behind my back because she knows that I dislike her sister. She may be afraid that I may say no. She comes from a family where they like to help each other."

When we asked him about other ways to handle the situation, he considered three different ways of discussing it with his wife:

1. "What bothers me is not that you help your sister, but that you do it behind my back."
2. "Why don't you keep a specific sum to spend as you wish."
3. "Maybe we should think about keeping separate savings accounts."

He also thought that he could walk out of the house to cool off, instead of pouring himself a drink.

Selecting the most promising approach: After weighing the consequences of each option, the client decided to talk to his wife, using options (1) and (2) above.

Assessing whether the new approach worked: The client was able to discuss the situation with his wife, as he had planned. They agreed that she would keep one-third of her salary to spend as she pleased.

Example 2: Temptation to give up

Another client was a 39-year-old woman who worked at the stock exchange. She drank heavily almost every weekend to cope with the pressures of her job and of raising three young children. She started the program because her drinking was affecting her health. When she completed the program, she had successfully achieved her goal of abstinence. But after three months of not drinking at all, she went on a very heavy drinking binge. She made an appointment with her counsellor because she was having doubts about herself and her success. She really didn't want to drink because of her health problems.

In considering her problem with binge drinking, she realized that the stress of her work had prompted her to drink as she had in the past. She felt guilty and ashamed, and began to have serious doubts about being able to maintain her goal of abstinence. She thought, "I will never make it. I am a failure. I'm not sure it is worth struggling so hard."

When her counsellor explored whether her negative thoughts were based in reality, she agreed that they were inaccurate and self-defeating. She was encouraged to see her binge-drinking episode in a more positive light. She realized that "One slip doesn't make me a failure. I can make it. I shouldn't be so hard on myself because of one slip." To cope with the pressures from work and home—without resorting to drinking—she decided to join a fitness club and plan outings with her children on weekends.

PRACTISE PROBLEM-SOLVING

Here are some scenarios often faced by people who are trying to quit or cut back on their drinking.

Some will apply to you more directly than others. Go through the steps of the problem-solving strategy and figure out how you would cope in each of the situations without drinking or over-drinking.

1. Imagine that you had a fight or disagreement with your spouse, your friend or your boss. This person accused you of not "pulling your weight," and took off without giving you the chance to discuss the situation. You thought the accusation was unjust. You became angry and were tempted to drink.

   How would you cope without drinking? Think about:
   - different ways to look at the situation and your emotional response to it
   - different ways to approach the person who made the accusation and to deal with the situation and resolve it—what would you say or do?

   Which options seem best?

2. Imagine that you are at a party. You are enjoying yourself, and no one is pressuring you to drink. Early in the evening, you find that you have reached your planned drinking limit. You do not want to leave, so you begin to make excuses to yourself to drink more.

   - How would you cope, without leaving the situation or over-drinking?
   - What would you say to yourself to counteract your excuses?
   - What would you do to avoid drinking too much?

3. Imagine that you are at a social function, and that your goal is abstinence. You see that most people around you are drinking, and they seem to be enjoying themselves. Your host approaches you several times to offer you a drink.

   - How would you refuse the offers without feeling uncomfortable?
   - What would you do to avoid offers from your host and other guests?

4. Imagine that you are 50 years old. You gave up a successful business to work for a well-established company. After several years of service, however, the company has gone broke; you have been laid off. At the time, you had been moderating your drinking successfully for one year.

   When the bad news comes you are shocked. You feel powerless, depressed, uncertain about the future. You begin to drink to cope with these feelings. You constantly have negative thoughts: "I will never be able to find another job like this one" or "Nobody will hire me again" or "I'm too old—I don't have the energy to go back to my old business." You worry that your spouse and your children will think you are incompetent.

   - What would you say to yourself to avoid drinking and to put yourself in a more positive frame of mind?
   - How would you go about looking at new job options?

Decision point

If you have not been drinking at all, or you have been moderating your drinking consistently for at least four weeks since you set your longer-term goal, CONGRATULATIONS!

Now you are ready to go to Step 5, which will give you the skills to maintain your goal.

However, if by the end of four to six weeks you have not consistently stayed within the limits you set, you should take some time to figure out why. Consider the following:

- Perhaps you should develop some additional strategies for the situations in which you did not meet your goal.
- Perhaps your problem is more serious than you thought.
- Perhaps you are not giving a high enough priority to this program as a way to moderate your drinking or abstain. Reassess why you want to change your drinking habits. Do you still see it as a very important goal in your life and one you want to accomplish at this time?

If you have closely followed the instructions in this guide, and it has not helped you to abstain or to develop a pattern of moderate drinking, think about seeing a professional. You may need more help than this guide can offer.

Step 5: Maintaining your progress

In this step we describe strategies that can help you to maintain abstinence or moderate drinking.

Proceed with this step if:
• you have reached your long-term goal
• you are confident that the goal you have reached is the goal you want to maintain.

To maintain your goal, you need to continue with the strategies you developed and practised in Step 4. You need to practise these strategies until they become automatic or "second nature." This process usually takes several months.

Strategies you have learned to maintain your long-term goal

KEEPING MY DRINKING DIARY

We urge you to continue to keep track of your drinking and abstinent days. Don't be tempted to give up keeping records after a few weeks. Remember, clients who keep records for several months tend to be much more successful in the long run. An accurate daily record is the best measure of your progress.

If you think you can stop monitoring your drinking and still stay within your limit, it is wise to keep track from time to time. This random check will confirm whether you are meeting your goal.

PACING MY DRINKING

If your goal is moderation, keep your wits about you: pace your drinking to avoid drinking too much. Do not forget to measure your drinks, try to dilute them and drink them slowly.

PLANNING AHEAD TO AVOID DRINKING MORE THAN MY LIMIT

Preparation is the key here. Remember, it is unwise to "play it by ear" when it comes to your own use of alcohol.

DEVELOPING LEISURE ACTIVITIES THAT DO NOT INVOLVE DRINKING

You need to make a deliberate effort to replace the time you spent drinking with other enjoyable and rewarding activities. Make drinking a secondary activity in your life.

COPING WITH MY PROBLEMS WITHOUT DRINKING

Use the problem-solving strategy on page 56 as soon as you face a problem, to help you overcome the negative feelings without drinking. Don't let your problems pile up.

Rule: Alcohol should not be used to cope with problems. If you experience problems that threaten your goal of moderate drinking or abstinence, try to find a positive solution as soon as possible. Do not let negative feelings build up. They can reactivate heavy drinking. If you feel you cannot tackle a problem on your own, seek help from family or friends, or from a professional.

More strategies to maintain your progress

DEALING WITH SLIPS RIGHT AWAY

Occasional slips—when you do not meet your goal, or when you drink too much—are not uncommon. Some clients got discouraged after a single slip and abandoned their goal. They may have thought, "It's useless to try" or "I'll never beat this problem." Don't use these negative feelings as an excuse to give up. If you drink too much, learn from your experience. Take a fresh look at your coping strategies and your goal.

GIVING MYSELF REGULAR CHECKUPS

Our clients reviewed their progress every three months.

Since you are working on your own, you will have to do your own follow-up. Set dates at three-month intervals over the next nine months to check your own progress. Make a note in your calendar, or wherever you record your appointments.

The date of my first checkup is _____

The date of my second checkup is _____

The date of my third checkup is _____

At each checkup, try to be objective about your progress. Ask yourself:
1. How much have I been drinking?
2. Has my drinking interfered in any way with my health or my responsibilities? If so, how should I adjust my goal to minimize risks?
3. Have I found enough activities that I find rewarding and enjoyable that do not involve drinking?

4. Am I coping effectively with urges to drink once I've reached my limit? What are my best strategies?

We have included four checkup forms in the Appendix (page 99) to help you keep track of the relevant information.

This completes the instructional part of the program.

CONGRATULATIONS!

Remember to keep your records and review your progress regularly.

COMMON QUESTIONS

In this section we answer five questions our clients often ask. Our responses take into account the most recent research evidence.

What is alcohol?

How much is too much?

Is "alcoholism" an inherited disease?

How do drinking habits develop?

How do people deal with drinking problems?

You don't need to read this section to start the program, but you should do so before completing it. We hope it will give you a better understanding of alcohol, how it affects you, and how this program aims to help you.

What is alcohol?

Alcohol is a drug that is naturally produced from the fermentation of fruits, vegetables or grains. There are many types of alcohol but the alcohol you find in drinks is ethyl alcohol or ethanol. We simply call it "alcohol." Alcohol has no real taste or smell. The tastes and smells of alcoholic beverages come from their food ingredients and added flavors.

Alcoholic beverages contain various concentrations of alcohol. Liquor has about 40 per cent, fortified wines such as sherry and vermouth have about 18 per cent, table wines vary between 10 and 14 per cent, and regular beer has about 5 per cent. Because of these differences, the concept of "standard drinks" was developed. Each standard drink contains the same amount of alcohol.

In Canada, one standard drink is:
341 mL (12 oz) of 5% alcohol **beer, cider or cooler**
142 mL (5 oz) of 12% alcohol **wine**
85 mL (3 oz) of 18% alcohol **fortified wine**
43 mL (1.5 oz) of 40% alcohol **liquor**.

Remember, a standard drink is a standard drink regardless of whether it comes in beer, wine or liquor. What affects you is not the type of beverage, but the amount of alcohol in your drink.

WHAT KIND OF DRUG IS ALCOHOL?

Some people believe that alcohol is a stimulant, since after a few drinks they become less inhibited and more talkative. In fact, alcohol is a depressant. It slows down the activity in your brain. This affects your mood, your ability to think and the way you behave.

Generally, one to two standard drinks will make you feel mildly relaxed. This relaxed feeling is particularly appealing in social gatherings or when you want to unwind from a hard day's work.

But when you drink too much, especially if you drink fast (that is, more than one drink per hour), the depressant effects of alcohol increase. You may slur your speech, have trouble walking, become confused, begin to act recklessly and do embarrassing things. If you drink a lot in a short period of time—for example, 10 to 15 drinks in one hour—you could go into a coma or even die. The bottom line is that drinking too much, or too quickly, is dangerous to your health and well-being.

But it is not just how much or how quickly you drink that has a direct bearing on how alcohol affects you. There are many other factors that are as important, for example:

• your age, sex and body weight
• the environment you're in
• how you expect alcohol to make you feel
• how sensitive you are to alcohol
• how long you've been drinking
• how often you drink
• whether you are drinking on a full or empty stomach
• whether you are tired
• whether you have taken other drugs or medications.

The effect alcohol has on you is determined by the combination of these factors. Therefore, it can be difficult to predict how alcohol will affect you at any given time.

HOW DOES YOUR BODY PROCESS ALCOHOL?

Alcohol is absorbed quickly from your stomach into your bloodstream. The blood then transports the alcohol to all regions of your body that have a high water content. These areas include your liver, brain, heart, lungs, pancreas, kidneys, spleen, reproductive organs, muscles, bone marrow and skin.

Your body starts removing alcohol as soon as it enters the bloodstream. Sweat, breath and urine remove a little, but a least 90 per cent is broken down and converted into other substances by the liver. It takes up to two hours for a healthy liver to break down one standard drink. This rate remains the same for every drink you have, no matter what you do— even if you eat, drink coffee or exercise.

The percentage of alcohol present in your blood is known as "blood alcohol concentration" or BAC for short. Your BAC and level of intoxication will rise depending on how much and how fast you drink.

If you are a woman, you are likely to reach a higher BAC than a man after drinking the same amount of alcohol. There are several reasons for this. One is that women's bodies are generally smaller than men's. Another is that a woman's body has less water than a man's to dilute the alcohol. And a third is that a woman's body processes alcohol more slowly.

The chart below shows the BACs of a man and a woman of average height and weight who have both consumed four standard drinks in two hours. The woman has a higher BAC than the man. Also, it takes the woman longer to eliminate the alcohol—six hours compared to about four hours for the man.

BLOOD ALCOHOL CONCENTRATION (BAC)
Comparison of male and female (same height, weight and drinks)

BAC g/100 mL (4 beers in 2 hours)

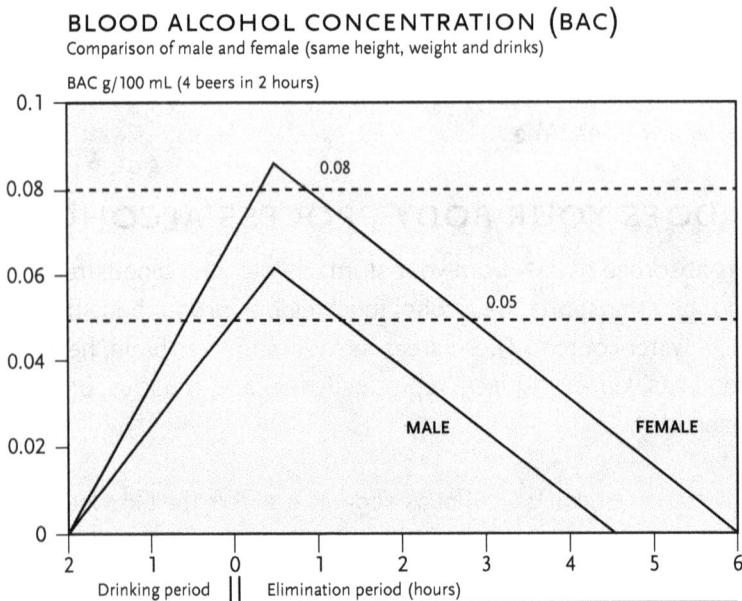

It is important for both men and women to be aware of the BAC levels that put them over the legal limit for driving. These limits vary by province and state. In Ontario, Canada, drivers caught with a BAC of .05 g/100mL can have their licence suspended and face other penalties. At a BAC over .08 g/100mL, a driver can be charged with impaired driving—a criminal offence.

Keep in mind that the only way to reduce your BAC level is to stop drinking or to pace yourself. Your body needs time to eliminate the alcohol.

IS ALCOHOL FATTENING?

If you are concerned about your weight or your diet, consider this: alcohol has many calories and no nutrients. The alcohol in one standard drink has about 100 calories. When you add a mix other than water, you are adding more calories. So whenever you drink, remember that you are consuming a lot of "empty" calories that have no nutritional value.

IS IT DANGEROUS TO MIX ALCOHOL WITH OTHER DRUGS?

Consuming alcohol when you have been taking other drugs—prescribed, over the counter or illegal—can have unpredictable results. Alcohol interacts with many drugs including antidepressants, stimulants and common medications. Even small amounts of alcohol combined with one of these drugs can severely affect your physical and mental abilities. Some medicines are less effective if you take them when you have alcohol in your body. Other medications if mixed with alcohol can cause side-effects such as cramps, vomiting and headaches. Therefore, the best advice is: DON'T MIX.

Combining alcohol with another depressant such as a sleeping pill or a tranquillizer may create a "synergistic" effect—the effect of both drugs will be increased and you may feel very intoxicated or even pass out.

Using stimulants such as caffeine, cocaine and amphetamines after you have been drinking may make you feel more alert. This may fool you into believing you are sober. The truth is you are still under the influence of alcohol. The popular belief that drinking strong coffee will sober you up is a myth—it's not true.

If you are using any prescription medications, check with your doctor or pharmacist about whether you should avoid drinking alcohol while taking the medicine.

How much is too much?

"Too much" is any drinking that interferes with your health, your relationships, your job or other responsibilities. It is also any drinking that threatens your safety and the safety of others.

But this question can be better answered if you ask:
• How much is too much for one occasion?
• How much is too much over a long period of time?

DRINKING TOO MUCH ON ONE OCCASION

There is no hard and fast rule about how much is too much on one occasion. It depends not only on the amount you drink and how quickly, but on the circumstances. For instance, it could be dangerous to drink any alcohol before you drive or operate heavy machinery, or while you take care of children. On the other hand, you could have several drinks at a family reunion in your home without experiencing any problems.

Drinking too much on one occasion can have many negative consequences. Some of them don't last long, such as a hangover or other unpleasant physical symptoms. But these symptoms can interfere with your responsibilities, or with your safety or the safety of others. If you turn to page 78 you will find a list of the negative consequences our clients experienced after drinking too much.

Other more serious consequences, such as traumatic injuries, happen when people have been drinking. Remember, a high blood alcohol concentration means you are likely to have poor co-ordination, poor judgment and drowsiness. This puts you at greater risk of accidents and other serious problems that can occur quickly, and with devastating impact.

DRINKING FREQUENTLY OVER A LONG PERIOD OF TIME

Drinking frequently over a long period of time also causes a wide range of problems. One of the most serious is a severe alcohol use disorder. Gradually, the cumulative effects of alcohol take their toll. For example, your liver can be damaged by heavy drinking. But it may take months or years before problems related to your drinking become apparent to you. Severe health problems can occur after many years of sustained frequent drinking (e.g., liver cirrhosis, stomach ulcers and some cancers).

Our clients typically reported drinking between five and seven drinks a day and had been experiencing problems for an average of five years. Their drinking had not yet caused them serious health problems, but it had caused them problems at home or work. These problems were likely to become very serious if they didn't change their drinking habits. When they came for treatment, our clients' alcohol use disorder was either mild or moderate—never severe. Those clients who had a severe alcohol use disorder were referred to appropriate programs.

The chart on page 74 illustrates some earlier consequences of heavy drinking and how they may develop into serious problems. People who drink heavily often experience several of these warning signs. They should take action before these signs evolve into serious problems.

Most of our clients had experienced several of the warning signs in the year before they started treatment. Reviewing this chart helped them to become more motivated about changing their drinking habits. Read the warning signs and see how many apply to you.

WARNING SIGNS	SERIOUS PROBLEMS
forgetting things	permanent memory impairment
abnormal results on liver function tests	liver cirrhosis
tolerance, craving, difficulty controlling alcohol use	addiction
stomach problems, such as nausea and vomiting	bleeding ulcer
family disputes about drinking	family breakup
missing work occasionally, late for work, or hungover at work	job loss
lower school grades	dropping out of school
reckless behaviour	injuring someone while drinking
driving after drinking	being charged with impaired driving
frequent heavy drinking	obsession with alcohol
spending too much money on alcohol	getting into debt
drinking to cope with stress	a severe alcohol use disorder

If you have experienced some of the warning signs in the past year, you are drinking too much and should take steps to change your drinking habits as soon as possible.

If you have experienced any of the serious problems in the past year, and you are still drinking, this program is not for you. You should seek professional help.

Is "alcoholism" an inherited disease?

About 40 per cent of our clients had one parent (usually their father) with a drinking problem. These clients were often concerned that they had an inherited disease. Perhaps they had read a story in the newspaper, watched a program on TV or talked to friends who have told them an alcohol problem may be "inherited." What follows is our response.

Certainly, "alcoholism," now referred to as "severe alcohol use disorder," is not a disease like the flu. It doesn't come from a germ you catch, or from a specific gene such as the one that produces colour blindness or Down Syndrome. Nonetheless, it is true that there are genetic aspects to severe alcohol use disorders. If you are a man, having a parent with a severe alcohol use disorder makes you four or five times more likely to develop an alcohol problem than the rest of the population. But it's important to remember that most men with a parent with an alcohol use disorder do *not* develop an alcohol problem themselves. Information about the incidence of alcohol use disorders in women who have a parent with an alcohol problem is scarce.

In cultures where alcohol is easily available, genetic and environmental factors have been shown to play a roughly equal role in the development of severe alcohol use disorders. In other words, where you live and who you spend time with have as much influence on whether you develop an alcohol use disorder as your genetics.

For biological reasons, some people are sensitive to the positive effects of alcohol and some are sensitive to the negative effects. It follows that a person who is sensitive to the positive effects of alcohol is at risk of heavy drinking. This is especially true in an environment where heavy drinking is the norm—for example, in the family or within a circle of friends. The risk is even higher if this person is also insensitive to the negative effects of alcohol, such as a hangover.

In contrast, a person who is sensitive to the negative effects of alcohol (such as nausea, numbness, dizziness, flushing and hangover) is biologically protected against heavy drinking. Even in people with biological protection, factors in the environment can override unpleasant effects. For example, someone may hate the taste of alcohol, but will drink heavily to numb a negative feeling.

Because a person's genetic makeup can influence his or her chance of developing a drinking problem, we encouraged our clients to take their family history into account when setting their goals. We pointed out that clients whose parents have had alcohol problems had been just as successful in our program. However, they were much more conservative when setting their goals for drinking.

How do drinking habits develop?

Have you asked yourself, "Why do I keep drinking the way I do, even when I know it's causing me problems?" Many of our clients have. In reply, we tell them about a simple model called the ABC's of Drinking: "A" stands for Activators, or the triggers of drinking. "B" is for Behaviours that lead to drinking. And "C" is for the Consequences of drinking.

It is easiest to describe this model if we start with C's and work back to the A's.

C'S—THE CONSEQUENCES OF DRINKING

Drinking has consequences that are viewed by the person as positive or negative. From studies of human learning, we know that habits develop because of their positive consequences. But to strengthen a habit, the positive consequences must follow the behaviour quickly and reliably. Each time you experience positive consequences of drinking, your habit is strengthened. It doesn't matter if the positive consequence is trivial or important—so long as it follows quickly and reliably, it will strengthen your habit.

If the positive consequences strengthen the habit, why don't the negative consequences of drinking drive the habit away? The answer: very serious negative consequences of drinking tend to be delayed and unreliable.

The chart on the next page shows examples of positive and negative consequences of drinking, and how quickly and reliably they occur.

TIMING OF CONSEQUENCE CHART

CONSEQUENCES	SECONDS/MINUTES	HOURS/DAYS	MONTHS/YEARS

POSITIVE

PHYSICAL
- good taste
- warmth
- relaxation
- relief of withdrawal
- sleepiness

PSYCHOSOCIAL
- confidence
- euphoria
- less anxious, bored, etc.

BEHAVIOURAL
- talkative
- flirtatious
- joking
- assertive
- loving

NEGATIVE

PHYSICAL

SECONDS/MINUTES	HOURS/DAYS	MONTHS/YEARS
• bad taste	• dizziness	• gastritis
	• nausea	• physical dependence
	• vomiting	• stomach ulcer
	• hangover	• liver disease
	• injury	• brain damage
		• cancer

PSYCHOSOCIAL

SECONDS/MINUTES	HOURS/DAYS	MONTHS/YEARS
• social disapproval	• embarrassment	• psychological dependence
	• guilt	• depression
	• self-disgust	• marital breakup
	• family conflict	• lower professional competence
	• impaired job performance	• job loss

BEHAVIOURAL

SECONDS/MINUTES	HOURS/DAYS	MONTHS/YEARS
	• aggression	• debt
	• over-spending	
	• impaired driving	
	• accidents	
	• legal charges	

As you can see, most positive consequences of drinking come within seconds or minutes. In contrast, any negative consequences are delayed—they come after hours, days, months or years—and often do not follow a specific episode of drinking.

People who decide to change their drinking habits usually do so because of a negative consequence. However, breaking the habit is a challenge because, as the desire to drink is triggered, the short-term positive effects of alcohol are the first to come to mind, not the longer-term negative consequences.

B'S—THE BEHAVIOURS OF DRINKING

Drinking behaviours become more and more elaborate as an alcohol use disorder develops. The B's of drinking are the chains of action that are completed predictably by people who consume alcohol.

Here are three examples:

John drinks lightly on occasion. You can only predict that John will drink if he actually has a drink in his hand. His drinking cannot be predicted by where he is, what he is doing or how he feels. So John has very few behaviours—or B's—associated with drinking.

Bill, on the other hand, drinks heavily and regularly. His drinking is much more predictable than John's. For example, if Bill leaves work with Dean, you can guarantee that in a few minutes the two will be sitting in the bar down the street having a drink. For Bill, one of the many B's of drinking is simply leaving work with Dean. Bill's other drinking behaviours include visiting his father-in-law and going curling with his buddies.

For Dean, there are even more B's of drinking. Entering the liquor store is one of them. If Dean goes into the liquor store, you can be sure that he will soon be taking a drink from the bottle he buys. By contrast, when John enters the liquor store, it is most likely that he's in the neighborhood and has taken the opportunity to make a purchase for a future occasion.

You cannot predict from the fact that John is in the liquor store that he will soon be taking a drink.

When you are trying to quit or cut down it is very important to identify the B's of your drinking. That's because it is easier to interrupt your behaviour chains when they are starting than when they are nearly completed.

A'S—THE ACTIVATORS OF DRINKING

The Activators of drinking are situations or events that trigger the desire to drink. They include your own feelings and thoughts, the sight and smell of alcohol, seeing people drink, watching a beer commercial on television, and so on.

We have identified three types of Activators:

1. **Unpleasant feelings that trigger drinking to cope.** Negative feelings may include anger, boredom, shyness and tension. Alcohol may alleviate these negative feelings or enable some kind of action. For example, many people who drink believe that interpersonal behaviours—such as making conversation, dancing, expressing opinions or having sex—become easier under the influence of alcohol.
2. **Situations in which people drink for pleasure.** Some situations reliably trigger the desire to drink for the "buzz" or enjoyment. This may be to celebrate something, to enhance the taste of a fine meal or to enjoy the taste of a favourite drink.
3. **Situations in which people drink out of habit.** Some people drink regularly in specific situations without giving it much thought, and independent of how they feel. Drinking out of habit starts as drinking for pleasure or to cope. But with repetition, drinking becomes almost automatic.

The Activators of drinking work like many other signals that start chains of behaviours almost automatically. For example, if the phone rings at your desk, you stop what you are doing and automatically lift the receiver. When driving, you automatically brake for a red light. You may be talking to someone at the time and not even notice the light consciously. Similarly, if the light is green you drive through without making any conscious decision that it is safe to go. You react to these signals without thinking. In situations where drinking has been very regular in the past, the A's—or Activators—of drinking can automatically trigger drinking behaviours—or B's.

A habit doesn't require much thought or concentration. An objective in this program is to get you to stop drinking without thinking. You will learn to recognize the A's, the B's and the C's of your drinking, and how to make any drinking a deliberate choice.

The diagram below illustrates the ABC's of drinking. Note that some C's can become Activators of further drinking, creating a "vicious circle." Negative emotions, hangovers and withdrawal are the consequences most likely to develop into A's of drinking.

For example, you argue with a friend while drinking. The next day, you're still feeling angry about the argument. You have a drink to cope with those feelings. Or you've got a bad hangover after a night of heavy drinking. It's only 9:00 a.m., but you think a quick drink will calm your nerves, make you feel a little better. . . .

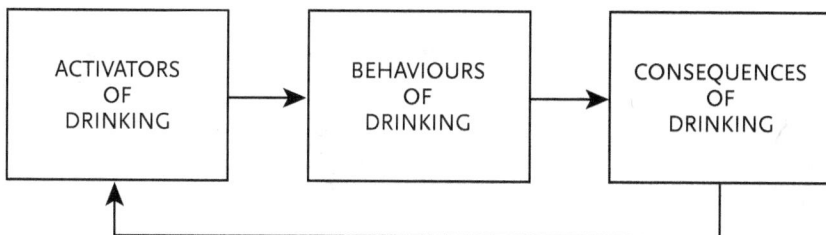

| ACTIVATORS OF DRINKING | → | BEHAVIOURS OF DRINKING | → | CONSEQUENCES OF DRINKING |

How do people deal with drinking problems?

Some people tackle their drinking problems on their own. Others turn to formal treatment or to mutual help groups such as Alcoholics Anonymous and Women for Sobriety.

Reasons why some people with drinking problems choose to "go it alone" rather than seek help may have to do with the stigma associated with seeking help, or believing that they have the skills to achieve problem-free drinking.

What motivates people to change their drinking habits? Sometimes, events in their lives make them reflect about the wisdom of continuing to drink as much. Some events are positive—getting married, starting a new job or entering parenthood. Others are negative—being charged for impaired driving, causing an accident, or experiencing a health problem or family conflict. Some people say that nothing specifically good or bad was happening in their lives when they decided to stop or cut down on their drinking. They simply got tired of the lifestyle that goes with frequent drinking.

DOING IT ON YOUR OWN

Almost 90 per cent of our clients had tried to curb their drinking before they came to treatment. This suggests that the first step for many people with drinking problems is to try to deal with their drinking on their own.

In our last study, we mailed an earlier version of this guide to people who wanted to quit or cut down on their own and welcomed a self-help guide. We asked those who were doing well one year later to tell us the steps they had taken to tackle their problem before they received the self-help materials.

They mentioned two strategies:
- keeping track by counting drinks and monitoring how much alcohol they were buying
- avoiding risky situations such as going into bars or socializing with people who drink heavily.

These two strategies are highly recommended in this guide.

MUTUAL HELP GROUPS

There are a variety of mutual help organizations for people with alcohol problems. Alcoholics Anonymous (AA) is by far the best known—it has millions of members worldwide. AA is free and welcomes anyone who wants to attend. Related programs provide support to the families of alcoholics.

The objective of AA is to help its members achieve sobriety—that is, complete abstinence from alcohol—and personal improvement. AA views "alcoholism" or a severe alcohol use disorder as a disease that is progressive and incurable. To halt the progression of the disease, "alcoholics" must stop drinking for the rest of their lives. Those who join AA are often experiencing severe alcohol problems.

The AA program consists of 12 steps, which each member accomplishes at his or her own pace. To do well in the program people should:
- accept the disease view of alcoholism
- accept that complete abstinence is the only way to arrest the disease
- attend meetings regularly
- progress through the 12 steps of the program.

FORMAL TREATMENT

Most substance use treatment programs accept the AA disease view of alcohol use disorders and the goal of sobriety for their patients. They often include three weeks of residential or day treatment followed by one or two years of regular aftercare. Treatment programs may be expensive, but in Canada their costs are usually covered by health insurance plans.

Treatment programs may make attendance at AA mandatory, but treatment includes many other elements, such as alcohol education, stress management and group therapy. Often, treatment programs require that family members or the employer be involved in the treatment process. A major objective is to teach those who are close to the client how to avoid covering up for him or her—or "enabling" the disease in other ways. Like AA, treatment programs tend to attract people who are experiencing severe alcohol problems.

PROGRAMS OF EARLY INTERVENTION

These programs are used with people who have less severe problems. The programs assume that drinking too much is a learned habit that can be changed by quitting or by cutting down.

The main objectives of the early intervention programs are to provide knowledge and teach skills that enable clients to avoid problems from drinking. The strategy is to attract people with less severe problems by incorporating features such as:
• considering problem drinking as a learned habit rather than a disease
• offering clients a choice of a goal—either abstinence or moderate drinking
• providing the opportunity to receive help without having to interrupt work or home responsibilities
• maximizing privacy—clients are not required to tell anyone that they are receiving help, or to involve others in the treatment process.

Programs of early intervention are relatively brief. Clients typically receive from three to six counselling sessions. The cost is sometimes covered by insurance plans; sometimes the user pays a fee. These programs can be offered by some college and university health centres, employee assistance programs, private therapists and community health clinics. Early intervention programs can also be found online, such as the one at Alcohol Help Center (www.alcoholhelpcenter.net).

This guide was developed out of our program of early intervention. The approach has worked for many people. We hope it is also helpful to you.

APPENDIX

Drinking Diary
Attached are enough forms to help you record your drinking for 23 weeks.

Coping Diary
Use these forms while you are trying to reach your goal.

Checkup forms
Use these forms to check your progress every three months.

Treatment resources
Whom to contact for more information about alcohol, other drugs and treatment programs.

Drinking Diary

Week (first)

MY GOAL FOR WEEK # _____

MAX # OF DRINKS PER DAY _____
MAX # OF DRINKING DAYS THIS WEEK _____
MAX # OF DRINKS THIS WEEK _____

DRINKING DIARY		M	T	W	T	F	S	S	
	# OF 12 OZ BOTTLES BEER								TOTAL # OF DRINKS THIS WEEK ▼
	# OF 5 OZ GLASSES WINE								
	# OF 3 OZ GLASSES FORT WINE*								
	# OF 1½ OZ SHOTS LIQUOR								
	TOTAL DRINKS PER DAY								

* FORT WINE (e.g., sherry, port, vermouth)

Week (second)

MY GOAL FOR WEEK # _____

MAX # OF DRINKS PER DAY _____
MAX # OF DRINKING DAYS THIS WEEK _____
MAX # OF DRINKS THIS WEEK _____

DRINKING DIARY		M	T	W	T	F	S	S	
	# OF 12 OZ BOTTLES BEER								TOTAL # OF DRINKS THIS WEEK ▼
	# OF 5 OZ GLASSES WINE								
	# OF 3 OZ GLASSES FORT WINE*								
	# OF 1½ OZ SHOTS LIQUOR								
	TOTAL DRINKS PER DAY								

* FORT WINE (e.g., sherry, port, vermouth)

Week (third)

MY GOAL FOR WEEK # _____

MAX # OF DRINKS PER DAY _____
MAX # OF DRINKING DAYS THIS WEEK _____
MAX # OF DRINKS THIS WEEK _____

DRINKING DIARY		M	T	W	T	F	S	S	
	# OF 12 OZ BOTTLES BEER								TOTAL # OF DRINKS THIS WEEK ▼
	# OF 5 OZ GLASSES WINE								
	# OF 3 OZ GLASSES FORT WINE*								
	# OF 1½ OZ SHOTS LIQUOR								
	TOTAL DRINKS PER DAY								

* FORT WINE (e.g., sherry, port, vermouth)

Week 1

MY GOAL FOR WEEK # _____

MAX # OF DRINKS PER DAY _____
MAX # OF DRINKING DAYS THIS WEEK _____
MAX # OF DRINKS THIS WEEK _____

DRINKING DIARY		M	T	W	T	F	S	S	TOTAL # OF DRINKS THIS WEEK ▼
	# OF 12 OZ BOTTLES BEER								
	# OF 5 OZ GLASSES WINE								
	# OF 3 OZ GLASSES FORT WINE*								
	# OF 1½ OZ SHOTS LIQUOR								
	TOTAL DRINKS PER DAY								

* FORT WINE (e.g., sherry, port, vermouth)

Week 2

MY GOAL FOR WEEK # _____

MAX # OF DRINKS PER DAY _____
MAX # OF DRINKING DAYS THIS WEEK _____
MAX # OF DRINKS THIS WEEK _____

DRINKING DIARY		M	T	W	T	F	S	S	TOTAL # OF DRINKS THIS WEEK ▼
	# OF 12 OZ BOTTLES BEER								
	# OF 5 OZ GLASSES WINE								
	# OF 3 OZ GLASSES FORT WINE*								
	# OF 1½ OZ SHOTS LIQUOR								
	TOTAL DRINKS PER DAY								

* FORT WINE (e.g., sherry, port, vermouth)

Week 3

MY GOAL FOR WEEK # _____

MAX # OF DRINKS PER DAY _____
MAX # OF DRINKING DAYS THIS WEEK _____
MAX # OF DRINKS THIS WEEK _____

DRINKING DIARY		M	T	W	T	F	S	S	TOTAL # OF DRINKS THIS WEEK ▼
	# OF 12 OZ BOTTLES BEER								
	# OF 5 OZ GLASSES WINE								
	# OF 3 OZ GLASSES FORT WINE*								
	# OF 1½ OZ SHOTS LIQUOR								
	TOTAL DRINKS PER DAY								

* FORT WINE (e.g., sherry, port, vermouth)

Week 4

MY GOAL FOR WEEK # _____

MAX # OF DRINKS PER DAY _____
MAX # OF DRINKING DAYS THIS WEEK _____
MAX # OF DRINKS THIS WEEK _____

DRINKING DIARY		M	T	W	T	F	S	S	TOTAL # OF DRINKS THIS WEEK ▼
	# OF 12 OZ BOTTLES BEER								
	# OF 5 OZ GLASSES WINE								
	# OF 3 OZ GLASSES FORT WINE*								
	# OF 1½ OZ SHOTS LIQUOR								
	TOTAL DRINKS PER DAY								

* FORT WINE (e.g., sherry, port, vermouth)

DRINKING DIARY

MY GOAL FOR WEEK # _____

MAX # OF DRINKS PER DAY _____
MAX # OF DRINKING DAYS THIS WEEK _____
MAX # OF DRINKS THIS WEEK _____

	M	T	W	T	F	S	S	
# OF 12 OZ BOTTLES BEER								TOTAL # OF DRINKS THIS WEEK ▼
# OF 5 OZ GLASSES WINE								
# OF 3 OZ GLASSES FORT WINE*								
# OF 1½ OZ SHOTS LIQUOR								
TOTAL DRINKS PER DAY								

* FORT WINE (e.g., sherry, port, vermouth)

DRINKING DIARY

MY GOAL FOR WEEK # _____

MAX # OF DRINKS PER DAY _____
MAX # OF DRINKING DAYS THIS WEEK _____
MAX # OF DRINKS THIS WEEK _____

	M	T	W	T	F	S	S	
# OF 12 OZ BOTTLES BEER								TOTAL # OF DRINKS THIS WEEK ▼
# OF 5 OZ GLASSES WINE								
# OF 3 OZ GLASSES FORT WINE*								
# OF 1½ OZ SHOTS LIQUOR								
TOTAL DRINKS PER DAY								

* FORT WINE (e.g., sherry, port, vermouth)

DRINKING DIARY

MY GOAL FOR WEEK # _____

MAX # OF DRINKS PER DAY _____
MAX # OF DRINKING DAYS THIS WEEK _____
MAX # OF DRINKS THIS WEEK _____

	M	T	W	T	F	S	S	
# OF 12 OZ BOTTLES BEER								TOTAL # OF DRINKS THIS WEEK ▼
# OF 5 OZ GLASSES WINE								
# OF 3 OZ GLASSES FORT WINE*								
# OF 1½ OZ SHOTS LIQUOR								
TOTAL DRINKS PER DAY								

* FORT WINE (e.g., sherry, port, vermouth)

DRINKING DIARY

MY GOAL FOR WEEK # _____

MAX # OF DRINKS PER DAY _____
MAX # OF DRINKING DAYS THIS WEEK _____
MAX # OF DRINKS THIS WEEK _____

	M	T	W	T	F	S	S	
# OF 12 OZ BOTTLES BEER								TOTAL # OF DRINKS THIS WEEK ▼
# OF 5 OZ GLASSES WINE								
# OF 3 OZ GLASSES FORT WINE*								
# OF 1½ OZ SHOTS LIQUOR								
TOTAL DRINKS PER DAY								

* FORT WINE (e.g., sherry, port, vermouth)

MY GOAL FOR WEEK # _____

MAX # OF DRINKS PER DAY _____
MAX # OF DRINKING DAYS THIS WEEK _____
MAX # OF DRINKS THIS WEEK _____

DRINKING DIARY		M	T	W	T	F	S	S	
	# OF 12 OZ BOTTLES BEER								TOTAL # OF DRINKS THIS WEEK ▼
	# OF 5 OZ GLASSES WINE								
	# OF 3 OZ GLASSES FORT WINE*								
	# OF 1½ OZ SHOTS LIQUOR								
	TOTAL DRINKS PER DAY								

* FORT WINE (e.g., sherry, port, vermouth)

MY GOAL FOR WEEK # _____

MAX # OF DRINKS PER DAY _____
MAX # OF DRINKING DAYS THIS WEEK _____
MAX # OF DRINKS THIS WEEK _____

DRINKING DIARY		M	T	W	T	F	S	S	
	# OF 12 OZ BOTTLES BEER								TOTAL # OF DRINKS THIS WEEK ▼
	# OF 5 OZ GLASSES WINE								
	# OF 3 OZ GLASSES FORT WINE*								
	# OF 1½ OZ SHOTS LIQUOR								
	TOTAL DRINKS PER DAY								

* FORT WINE (e.g., sherry, port, vermouth)

MY GOAL FOR WEEK # _____

MAX # OF DRINKS PER DAY _____
MAX # OF DRINKING DAYS THIS WEEK _____
MAX # OF DRINKS THIS WEEK _____

DRINKING DIARY		M	T	W	T	F	S	S	
	# OF 12 OZ BOTTLES BEER								TOTAL # OF DRINKS THIS WEEK ▼
	# OF 5 OZ GLASSES WINE								
	# OF 3 OZ GLASSES FORT WINE*								
	# OF 1½ OZ SHOTS LIQUOR								
	TOTAL DRINKS PER DAY								

* FORT WINE (e.g., sherry, port, vermouth)

MY GOAL FOR WEEK # _____

MAX # OF DRINKS PER DAY _____
MAX # OF DRINKING DAYS THIS WEEK _____
MAX # OF DRINKS THIS WEEK _____

DRINKING DIARY		M	T	W	T	F	S	S	
	# OF 12 OZ BOTTLES BEER								TOTAL # OF DRINKS THIS WEEK ▼
	# OF 5 OZ GLASSES WINE								
	# OF 3 OZ GLASSES FORT WINE*								
	# OF 1½ OZ SHOTS LIQUOR								
	TOTAL DRINKS PER DAY								

* FORT WINE (e.g., sherry, port, vermouth)

Appendix

MY GOAL FOR WEEK # _____

MAX # OF DRINKS PER DAY _____
MAX # OF DRINKING DAYS THIS WEEK _____
MAX # OF DRINKS THIS WEEK _____

DRINKING DIARY		M	T	W	T	F	S	S	
	# OF 12 OZ BOTTLES BEER								TOTAL # OF DRINKS THIS WEEK ▼
	# OF 5 OZ GLASSES WINE								
	# OF 3 OZ GLASSES FORT WINE*								
	# OF 1½ OZ SHOTS LIQUOR								
	TOTAL DRINKS PER DAY								

* FORT WINE (e.g., sherry, port, vermouth)

MY GOAL FOR WEEK # _____

MAX # OF DRINKS PER DAY _____
MAX # OF DRINKING DAYS THIS WEEK _____
MAX # OF DRINKS THIS WEEK _____

DRINKING DIARY		M	T	W	T	F	S	S	
	# OF 12 OZ BOTTLES BEER								TOTAL # OF DRINKS THIS WEEK ▼
	# OF 5 OZ GLASSES WINE								
	# OF 3 OZ GLASSES FORT WINE*								
	# OF 1½ OZ SHOTS LIQUOR								
	TOTAL DRINKS PER DAY								

* FORT WINE (e.g., sherry, port, vermouth)

MY GOAL FOR WEEK # _____

MAX # OF DRINKS PER DAY _____
MAX # OF DRINKING DAYS THIS WEEK _____
MAX # OF DRINKS THIS WEEK _____

DRINKING DIARY		M	T	W	T	F	S	S	
	# OF 12 OZ BOTTLES BEER								TOTAL # OF DRINKS THIS WEEK ▼
	# OF 5 OZ GLASSES WINE								
	# OF 3 OZ GLASSES FORT WINE*								
	# OF 1½ OZ SHOTS LIQUOR								
	TOTAL DRINKS PER DAY								

* FORT WINE (e.g., sherry, port, vermouth)

MY GOAL FOR WEEK # _____

MAX # OF DRINKS PER DAY _____
MAX # OF DRINKING DAYS THIS WEEK _____
MAX # OF DRINKS THIS WEEK _____

DRINKING DIARY		M	T	W	T	F	S	S	
	# OF 12 OZ BOTTLES BEER								TOTAL # OF DRINKS THIS WEEK ▼
	# OF 5 OZ GLASSES WINE								
	# OF 3 OZ GLASSES FORT WINE*								
	# OF 1½ OZ SHOTS LIQUOR								
	TOTAL DRINKS PER DAY								

* FORT WINE (e.g., sherry, port, vermouth)

MY GOAL FOR WEEK # _____

MAX # OF DRINKS PER DAY _____
MAX # OF DRINKING DAYS THIS WEEK _____
MAX # OF DRINKS THIS WEEK _____

DRINKING DIARY		M	T	W	T	F	S	S	TOTAL # OF DRINKS THIS WEEK ▼
	# OF 12 OZ BOTTLES BEER								
	# OF 5 OZ GLASSES WINE								
	# OF 3 OZ GLASSES FORT WINE*								
	# OF 1½ OZ SHOTS LIQUOR								
	TOTAL DRINKS PER DAY								

* FORT WINE (e.g., sherry, port, vermouth)

MY GOAL FOR WEEK # _____

MAX # OF DRINKS PER DAY _____
MAX # OF DRINKING DAYS THIS WEEK _____
MAX # OF DRINKS THIS WEEK _____

DRINKING DIARY		M	T	W	T	F	S	S	TOTAL # OF DRINKS THIS WEEK ▼
	# OF 12 OZ BOTTLES BEER								
	# OF 5 OZ GLASSES WINE								
	# OF 3 OZ GLASSES FORT WINE*								
	# OF 1½ OZ SHOTS LIQUOR								
	TOTAL DRINKS PER DAY								

* FORT WINE (e.g., sherry, port, vermouth)

MY GOAL FOR WEEK # _____

MAX # OF DRINKS PER DAY _____
MAX # OF DRINKING DAYS THIS WEEK _____
MAX # OF DRINKS THIS WEEK _____

DRINKING DIARY		M	T	W	T	F	S	S	TOTAL # OF DRINKS THIS WEEK ▼
	# OF 12 OZ BOTTLES BEER								
	# OF 5 OZ GLASSES WINE								
	# OF 3 OZ GLASSES FORT WINE*								
	# OF 1½ OZ SHOTS LIQUOR								
	TOTAL DRINKS PER DAY								

* FORT WINE (e.g., sherry, port, vermouth)

MY GOAL FOR WEEK # _____

MAX # OF DRINKS PER DAY _____
MAX # OF DRINKING DAYS THIS WEEK _____
MAX # OF DRINKS THIS WEEK _____

DRINKING DIARY		M	T	W	T	F	S	S	TOTAL # OF DRINKS THIS WEEK ▼
	# OF 12 OZ BOTTLES BEER								
	# OF 5 OZ GLASSES WINE								
	# OF 3 OZ GLASSES FORT WINE*								
	# OF 1½ OZ SHOTS LIQUOR								
	TOTAL DRINKS PER DAY								

* FORT WINE (e.g., sherry, port, vermouth)

Coping Diary

DETAILS OF MY URGE TO DRINK

Time of day _____ Place _____ I was with _____

My feelings _____

_____

HOW I HANDLED IT

This is what I said to myself _____

_____

This is what I did to cope _____

_____

This is how I said 'no' when I was invited to drink _____

_____

DID MY COPING STRATEGY WORK? ☐ Yes ☐ No

DETAILS OF MY URGE TO DRINK

Time of day _____ Place _____ I was with _____

My feelings _____

_____

HOW I HANDLED IT

This is what I said to myself _____

_____

This is what I did to cope _____

_____

This is how I said 'no' when I was invited to drink _____

_____

DID MY COPING STRATEGY WORK? ☐ Yes ☐ No

DETAILS OF MY URGE TO DRINK

Time of day _____ Place _____ I was with _____

My feelings_____

_____

HOW I HANDLED IT

This is what I said to myself _____

_____

This is what I did to cope _____

_____

This is how I said 'no' when I was invited to drink _____

_____

DID MY COPING STRATEGY WORK? ☐ Yes ☐ No

COPING DIARY

DETAILS OF MY URGE TO DRINK

Time of day _____ Place _____ I was with _____

My feelings_____

_____

HOW I HANDLED IT

This is what I said to myself _____

_____

This is what I did to cope _____

_____

This is how I said 'no' when I was invited to drink _____

_____

DID MY COPING STRATEGY WORK? ☐ Yes ☐ No

COPING DIARY

DETAILS OF MY URGE TO DRINK

Time of day _____ Place _____ I was with _____

My feelings_____

_____

HOW I HANDLED IT

This is what I said to myself _____

_____

This is what I did to cope _____

_____

This is how I said 'no' when I was invited to drink _____

_____

DID MY COPING STRATEGY WORK? ☐ Yes ☐ No

COPING DIARY

DETAILS OF MY URGE TO DRINK

Time of day _____ Place _____ I was with _____

My feelings_____

_____

HOW I HANDLED IT

This is what I said to myself _____

_____

This is what I did to cope _____

_____

This is how I said 'no' when I was invited to drink _____

_____

DID MY COPING STRATEGY WORK? ☐ Yes ☐ No

COPING DIARY

DETAILS OF MY URGE TO DRINK

Time of day _____ Place _____ I was with _____

My feelings_____

_____

HOW I HANDLED IT

This is what I said to myself _____

_____

This is what I did to cope _____

_____

This is how I said 'no' when I was invited to drink _____

_____

DID MY COPING STRATEGY WORK? ☐ Yes ☐ No

COPING DIARY

DETAILS OF MY URGE TO DRINK

Time of day _____ Place _____ I was with _____

My feelings_____

_____

HOW I HANDLED IT

This is what I said to myself _____

_____

This is what I did to cope _____

_____

This is how I said 'no' when I was invited to drink _____

_____

DID MY COPING STRATEGY WORK? ☐ Yes ☐ No

COPING DIARY

DETAILS OF MY URGE TO DRINK

Time of day _____ Place _____ I was with _____

My feelings_____

_____

HOW I HANDLED IT

This is what I said to myself _____

_____

This is what I did to cope _____

_____

This is how I said 'no' when I was invited to drink _____

_____

DID MY COPING STRATEGY WORK? ☐ Yes ☐ No

DETAILS OF MY URGE TO DRINK

Time of day _____ Place _____ I was with _____

My feelings_____

_____

HOW I HANDLED IT

This is what I said to myself _____

_____

This is what I did to cope _____

_____

This is how I said 'no' when I was invited to drink _____

_____

DID MY COPING STRATEGY WORK? ☐ Yes ☐ No

DETAILS OF MY URGE TO DRINK

Time of day _____ Place _____ I was with _____

My feelings_____

_____

HOW I HANDLED IT

This is what I said to myself _____

_____

This is what I did to cope _____

_____

This is how I said 'no' when I was invited to drink _____

_____

DID MY COPING STRATEGY WORK? ☐ Yes ☐ No

COPING DIARY

COPING DIARY

COPING DIARY

Checkup 1

Period covered: _____

SUMMARY OF MY DRINKING—28-DAY PERIOD

	Number of days (A)	Typical number of drinks (B)	Totals (A x B)
Days with no drinking	_____		
Days with 1–4 drinks	_____	x _____	= _____
Days with 5–9 drinks	_____	x _____	= _____
Days with 10 or more drinks	_____	x _____	= _____

(= 28 days)   Total drinks (28 days) _____

Weekly Average (total drinks ÷ 4 weeks) _____

COPING WITH URGES TO DRINK OVER MY GOAL

My best ways of saying "NO" to myself: _____

_____

_____

_____

My best ways of saying "NO" to others when they invite me to drink:

_____

_____

_____

My most useful activities to avoid heavy drinking: _____

_____

_____

_____

Checkup 2

Period covered: _____

SUMMARY OF MY DRINKING—28-DAY PERIOD

	Number of days (A)	Typical number of drinks (B)	Totals (A x B)
Days with no drinking	_____		
Days with 1–4 drinks	_____	x _____	= _____
Days with 5–9 drinks	_____	x _____	= _____
Days with 10 or more drinks	_____	x _____	= _____

(= 28 days)   Total drinks (28 days) _____

Weekly Average (total drinks ÷ 4 weeks) _____

COPING WITH URGES TO DRINK OVER MY GOAL

My best ways of saying "NO" to myself: _____

_____
_____
_____

My best ways of saying "NO" to others when they invite me to drink:

_____
_____
_____

My most useful activities to avoid heavy drinking: _____

_____
_____
_____

Checkup 3

Period covered: _____

SUMMARY OF MY DRINKING—28-DAY PERIOD

	Number of days (A)	Typical number of drinks (B)	Totals (A x B)
Days with no drinking	_____		
Days with 1–4 drinks	_____	x _____	= _____
Days with 5–9 drinks	_____	x _____	= _____
Days with 10 or more drinks	_____	x _____	= _____

(= 28 days)   Total drinks (28 days) _____

Weekly Average (total drinks ÷ 4 weeks) _____

COPING WITH URGES TO DRINK OVER MY GOAL

My best ways of saying "NO" to myself: _____
_____
_____
_____

My best ways of saying "NO" to others when they invite me to drink:
_____
_____
_____

My most useful activities to avoid heavy drinking: _____
_____
_____
_____

Checkup 4

Period covered: _____

SUMMARY OF MY DRINKING—28-DAY PERIOD

	Number of days (A)		Typical number of drinks (B)		Totals (A x B)
Days with no drinking	_____				
Days with 1–4 drinks	_____	x	_____	=	_____
Days with 5–9 drinks	_____	x	_____	=	_____
Days with 10 or more drinks	_____	x	_____	=	_____

(= 28 days)   Total drinks (28 days) _____

Weekly Average (total drinks ÷ 4 weeks) _____

COPING WITH URGES TO DRINK OVER MY GOAL

My best ways of saying "NO" to myself: _____
_____
_____
_____

My best ways of saying "NO" to others when they invite me to drink:
_____
_____
_____

My most useful activities to avoid heavy drinking: _____
_____
_____
_____

Treatment resources

If you need more information about problems related to your alcohol use, you can start by talking to someone you trust—such as a doctor, nurse, counsellor, therapist, social worker, employee health officer, or anyone else you have faith in.

You may also consider contacting mutual-help groups such as Alcoholics Anonymous (AA). To find an AA group in your community, check their directory online.

www.aa.org. Click on How to find AA meetings.

To find addiction treatment services in your community, you can also check with the organizations listed below.

IN CANADA

Canadian Centre for Substance Abuse (CCSA)

This national organization provides a list of helplines and contact numbers for addiction treatment in your province or territory, and also a database of all treatment resources in Canada.

www.ccsa.ca/Eng/Topics/Treatment/default/Pages/default.aspx

IN THE UNITED STATES

Substance Abuse and Mental Health Services Administration (SAMHSA)

Call SAMHSA's 24-hour toll-free treatment referral helpline at 1 800 662-HELP (1 800 662-4357) or search online for a facility in your community.

http://samhsa.gov/treatment

ABOUT THE AUTHOR

As a senior scientist with the Addiction Research Foundation in Toronto, Canada, for more than 20 years, Dr. Martha Sanchez-Craig evaluated a variety of treatment methods for patients whose alcohol problems range from mild to severe. Treatment goals for her patients included abstinence and moderate drinking. Dr. Sanchez-Craig studied undergraduate psychology and philosophy in Mexico and holds a PhD in Counselling Psychology from the University of Toronto. Dr Sanchez-Craig is now happily retired.

www.ingramcontent.com/pod-product-compliance
Lightning Source LLC
Chambersburg PA
CBHW052042270326
41931CB00012B/2595